YOUR MUSEUM NEEDS A PODCAST

Hannah Hethmon

A Step-By-Step Guide to Podcasting on a Budget
for Museums, History Organizations, and Cultural Nonprofits

Download the Audiobook Free!

Just to say thank you for buying my book, I would like to give you the audiobook version 100% for free!

Visit **http://hhethmon.com/BookBonus**
to download the audiobook.

Ready to Start Engaging Your Audience through the Power of Podcasting?

Let me get you off to a great start and keep you on the right track from concept to launch (and beyond) with services tailored to the unique needs of museums, history organizations, libraries, religious organizations, and cultural nonprofits.

As an award-winning podcaster with experience in public history and museums, I can help your organization use the power of podcasting to meaningfully engage your audience.

Book a free 15-minute call and let's get your podcast project on track to meet your goals.

Contents

ACKNOWLEDGMENTS

I couldn't have written this without the constant support of two key people: my husband, Aleksi Korpela, and my incredible mom, Lori Hethmon. Thanks for believing in me! Thank you to my dear friend Scott Coffey for designing this amazing cover. A huge thank-you to the folks at the American Association for State and Local History (AASLH); those years working to serve history organizations ended up being a crash course in public history and museum administration. Thank you to the Fulbright Program for giving me the once-in-a-lifetime opportunity to spend nine months in Iceland working on my podcast. And finally, thanks to all the supportive podcasters I've met in the She Podcasts and Podcast Movement communities; I am constantly amazed by how generously you have shared your time and expertise with me as I learned the ropes.

Introduction

I believe museums, history organizations, and cultural nonprofits have the potential to change the world by making people more empathetic, creating connected communities, and by—collectively—safeguarding our autobiographies of place and identity.

I believe podcasting can be a powerful tool for museums, history organizations, and cultural nonprofits to reach their audiences and communicate in ways that are creative, intimate, and meaningful. In fact, these institutions already have the skills and information needed to make great podcasts.

However, there's a barrier to entry for organizations that want to join the growing world of podcasting, and if you've been looking for resources to learn how to podcast, you've probably already guessed what it is.

Of all the thousands of resources available to aspiring podcasters, only a handful are tailored to the unique needs of museums and related institutions. Most podcasting resources out there are geared towards people who want to create talk-show-style interview podcasts or money-making podcasts.

The cultural nonprofit world needed a comprehensive guide to podcasting written just for our unique needs, and that's what I am offering in these pages.

What's in the Book?

The chapters in this book will take you through everything you need to know to launch a podcast that accomplishes your organization's goals. I'll walk you through the whole process, from deciding what to podcast about and creating a budget to hosting, publishing, and marketing your show.

I've written this book for institutions who want to produce a show in-house. Those of you intending to outsource some or all of the production should read it as well, so that you can make more informed decisions about who you hire and which aspects of podcasting you want to outsource.

Every section is written with your budget in mind. I've focused on getting you the best sound and impact for a very low financial investment.

(By the way, for the purposes of this book, I'm defining podcasts as serialized audio distributed online through an RSS feed, not video or audio only posted on a website. While these latter mediums may still technically be considered "podcasts" by many, the popular definition and medium is the former.)

Unsure of what equipment you really need to get started? In "Chapter 2: Equipment and Software," I recommend the best mics and equipment for different purposes, so you don't need to spend weeks becoming a tech expert and trying to figure out the difference between a condenser mic and a dynamic mic.

Just reading those last few words will stress many of you out. Don't worry. The equipment chapter of this book is for people who want to make an educated decision on mics and recorders but aren't able or willing to wade through hundreds of different opinions on the internet.

In each chapter of the book, you'll get simple, concise advice and instruction that gives you just what you need to get started, without any treatises on sound engineering or editing. To make podcasting accessible to busy professionals in this field, I've left out all the unnecessary stuff so that you can just read the book, follow my instructions, and get started without breaking the bank or wasting hours wading through incomplete instructions on the internet.

You may be wondering if you can actually pull this off without any previous podcasting experience. The answer is yes. I know because I've already done it.

When I started *Museums in Strange Places*, I hadn't used a microphone more than once or twice in my life. I just had an idea to podcast about exploring the world through its museums and the confidence to try. I started with the recommendations of another podcaster in the museum world, spent $300 on equipment, moved to Iceland for a Fulbright Fellowship, and started sending emails asking the staff at Icelandic museums if I could interview them.

I started with far less information than you will have if you read this book, but in less than a year, I developed an international audience, reached download numbers that put me in the top 50% of podcast listenership, won an award from the American Alliance of Museums, and secured multiple sponsors to support the podcast.

The truth is that most podcasters have to learn "on the job." There's no centralized training program for podcasting, and even the best podcasters have had to just figure things out by asking questions, experimenting, and making episode after episode. But you have an advantage because I'm going to spell out for you everything you need to consider before making your first episode.

The bottom line is that I'm "unqualified," your favorite podcaster is probably "unqualified," and you are "unqualified." The only thing that separates podcasters from people who just talk about starting a podcast is that podcasters take the plunge and don't let their fears of failure or qualifications hold them back.

Why Podcasting?

The recent boom in podcast listening and creation presents a unique opportunity for museums, history organizations, and cultural nonprofits to regularly reach their visitors and community members at home, during their commute, or even at work.

Podcasting is an incredibly intimate medium. After all, you're speaking directly into your listener's ear. Listeners' favorite podcasters become part of their daily life and routine—someone they trust to entertain them, inform them, and keep them company.

In a world where it feels impossible to keep anyone's attention online for more than a few seconds, podcast fans are bucking the trend of constant distraction by listening loyally to entire episodes from their favorite shows, not flipping through channels to find something that catches their attention. Edison Research's *2018 Infinite Dial Study* revealed that 80% of podcast listeners hear all or most of each episode they consume.

What would you say if you could speak directly to your target audience for thirty minutes without any interruption?

Once you have your audience's attention, anything is possible. You can increase visitor rates, ask for donations, find volunteers, or become a place that people talk about and think about on a regular basis—instead of somewhere they just visit once or twice in as many years.

The proof is in the podcasts that are already out there. The big museums with marketing departments and eyes on the future of media are already podcasting or trying to get into the medium. From the MoMA in New York City to the Smithsonian Institution in Washington, D.C. to the British Museum in London to the Australian Museum in Sydney, the power of podcasting for cultural institutions is becoming common knowledge.

Museums that have been trying to share their collections and engage audiences online have realized that it's an uphill battle getting readers to sit down and actually finish a blog post. That is, if readers can even find the museum blog among the 500 million other blogs online.[1]

---

[1] In 2017, there were 440 million blogs on just Wordpress, Squarespace, and Tumblr alone. So, the actual number is probably much higher. "How Many Blogs

The podcast field, however, is wide open and there's plenty of room for new and exciting shows. It's a lot easier to find your niche among the 550,000 podcasts out there than an ocean of blogs. Plus, it's a medium perfectly suited to the shorter attention spans of readers as well as the on-the-go lifestyle of millennials and other working generations.

The podcast boom is happening *now*. Every year, more people listen to more podcasts, and more brands and nonprofit institutions are seeing how this medium can offer them direct access to their audience. Thanks in large part to the podcast *Serial*, podcast listening is mainstream, and discussing which podcasts you've binged recently is water-cooler talk.

This is exciting! But it's also a sign that if you are considering starting a podcast for your institution, now is the time to start. Not next year, not when you know enough, but *now*.

Here's how to get started: read this book, pitch a podcast to your boss or stakeholders using the templates and worksheets included with the book, and start reaching current and new audiences wherever they are with accessible engaging podcast episodes.

To help you implement some of the strategies and techniques I describe in these pages, I've created a bundle of easy-to-use worksheets and templates. Download them for FREE by visiting http://hhethmon.com/BookBonus and entering your email.

What are you waiting for? Turn the page, and let's get your podcast started!

Are There In The World?" Mediakix. September 14, 2017.
http://mediakix.com/2017/09/how-many-blogs-are-there-in-the-world/.

Chapter 1
Refining Your Show Idea

Planning makes everything better. Before you can begin working on the technical elements of your podcast, you have to refine your idea and know where it's heading. If you just start recording this and that without a clear goal, your podcast will not be successful. In this chapter, I'm going to lay out different strategies for refining your idea into a show concept that will best serve your institutional strategy and engage listeners.

Defining Your Audience

The very first thing you need to ask yourself before choosing a concept for your podcast is this: "Who is my audience?"

If you are creating a personal passion project out of your home studio and don't care if anyone listens to your podcast, it's okay to just pick a show idea and run with it. But if you are creating a podcast for an institution in order to meet certain goals, you must spell out clearly who will be listening to this podcast.

Remember that not everyone listens to podcasts. The listener base is large and growing every day, but you won't be able to suddenly change the makeup of podcast fans with your show, so it's worth taking a look at these statistics about podcast listeners today:[2]

---

[2] Statistics are from March 2018 and compiled by Podcast Insights (https://www.podcastinsights.com/podcast-statistics/)

- Podcast listeners are loyal, affluent, and educated.
- Podcast listeners are 56% men, 44% women.
- 45% of monthly podcast listeners have household income over $75K (vs 35% for the total population).
- 49% of podcast listening is done at home and 22% while driving.
- Podcast listeners are much more active on every social media channel (94% are active on at least one vs 81% for the entire population).
- Podcast listeners are more likely to follow companies and brands on social media.
- 69% agreed that podcast ads made them aware of new products or services.

How can you identify *your* audience? If your organization has data or research on your visitors or community members, that's a great place to start looking for the answer to this question. If there's no existing research, write down what you know about your current audience. Try answering these questions about the people who are the *most engaged* with your institution:

- How old are they?
- Economic status? Political affiliation? Race or ethnicity?
- When and how do they visit the museum or attend your programs?
- Where do they live?
- What keeps them up at night?
- What do they do for fun?
- What are they interested in?
- What do they love the most about your institution?
- What do they want to listen to?

If you feel stumped by that final question, get some answers by asking your social media followers to share their favorite podcasts, surveying visitors at the door, or asking people on your email list to help you develop a podcast concept by answering a few questions about their listening habits and favorite shows. Again, not everyone listens to podcasts, so you'll have more success building your podcast concept around the folks in your audience who are already podcast consumers because they are much more likely to start listening to your show when it launches.

Once you have some notes or research gathered, create a profile of your listener, an avatar that you can build the show idea around. Of course, not everyone who listens will be like this avatar, but creating the profile will help you identify which segments of your existing audience are likely to listen to your institution's podcast. Post this avatar profile up on the wall or somewhere you'll see it when you start writing scripts and marketing your podcast. These are two key points when you need to write *for* someone, and that someone should be your avatar or target audience.

This may be hard to hear, but I can say with 100% certainty that "all our visitors" is not your podcast audience. "Anyone in the world interested in history" is also not your audience. Your podcast should be created for a specific niche of listeners who cannot find what you are offering anywhere else.

I know that broad appeal is a tempting goal, but if you try to appeal to everyone, you'll set yourself up for failure and end up engaging no one. In order to win a coveted spot on the list of shows your audience follows loyally, you will have to stand out. General interest doesn't stand out; there's got to be a hook.

I'll dive a bit deeper into how focused your show should be and how to find your hook later in this chapter, but first, it's time to step back and think big-picture about the outcomes your museum, history organization, or cultural institution wants or needs to achieve as a result of this podcast project.

Setting Goals

I'm guessing you don't usually put on exhibits or launch public programs just because a staff member wants to try it or because it sounds fun. Of course you don't. You have a more in-depth process to evaluate how the program will further your institutional mission, meet a community's needs, or raise money to keep the doors open.

A podcast should not be any different. You need to know what you want to achieve before you can confidently decide what to podcast about.

Do you already have an outcome in mind? Or has one already been assigned to the project? If so, write it down now, before we go any further.

If you don't already have outcomes in mind, grab your institution's most recent strategic plan, any documents used in evaluating exhibit or program ideas, or at the very least re-read your mission statement. How can a podcast answer some of the needs expressed in these documents?

- Will it increase visitor rates?
- Will it build the local community?
- Will it increase awareness of your mission?
- Will it educate listeners?
- Will it entertain your audience?
- Will it teach a needed skill or concept to your audience?
- Will it provide a platform for expression of a minority voice?
- Will it make your institution a regular part of your audience's lives?
- Will it raise your local or international profile?
- Will it fill a need in your audience's lives?
- Will it open doors to new avenues of community outreach?
- Will it help raise money for the organization?

These are important questions to ask yourself because if you are going to successfully pitch a podcast to your superiors, stakeholders, or board members, you must be able to express how the podcast fits into the big picture and why it's worth an investment of time and money.

If you are starting to feel overwhelmed by the pre-planning or anxious wondering how to pitch your podcast project, don't worry. In the *Worksheet and Template Bundle* available at http://hhethmon.com/BookBonus, there are a set of templates and worksheets created to make planning and pitching easy. You may want to download those as word documents now and use them to take notes while you read the book.

Before we move on to talking more about types of podcasts and other information that will help you figure out how a podcast fits into your institution's larger strategic goals, I want to state firmly that podcasts are not just advertisements. If you start the podcast with the main intention of telling people where you are located and when you are open, you will not see great results.

Podcasting is all about creating engaging audio shows that listeners want to hear. You will need to explain how a podcast can help meet goals, but the way it will meet those goals should always be by creating unique, thoughtful episodes that stand on their own merit and can be enjoyed even if the listener never visits your exhibits or signs up for your programs.

If your only goal is to advertise an exhibit or event, you can do that by putting up a billboard or taking out ads somewhere. Podcasting is a very ineffective way to simply share advertisements. Listeners expect more from podcasts; using them as a way to sneak advertisements into your audience's podcast player is not a good way to engage your audience.

Types of Podcasts

There are so many kinds of podcasts out there. It's a medium that allows for innovation and experimentation, which means the possibilities are endless. But a few general types of podcasts are most common. Let's break those down to see which is the best fit for your institution.

First, I want to make it clear that many podcasts are hybrids of these types. You do not under any circumstances have to pick just one or the other for your show concept. You can have an audio drama that's a fake talk show or a co-hosted show where you discuss pre-recorded interviews. These types are just here to help you explore all the possibilities.

Interview & Talk Show Podcasts

This is probably the most common and widely recognized format for podcasts. There are many different varieties, but the common factor is two or more people sitting in a studio talking to each other. You can probably think of any number of television and radio shows that use this format, whether it's three co-hosts discussing the latest celebrity news or Terry Gross interviewing a guest on *Fresh Air*. You can also take an interview show to the streets, interviewing guests at their jobs, in their homes, or on the go.

Though it's one of the simplest frameworks for creating a podcast, interviewing guests and generating engaging dialogue between co-hosts takes practice. In the host and guest format, it's up to the interviewer to keep the conversation fresh and focused, even when the guest is boring or having a bad day. Many people who are sparkling conversationalists off-air just completely clam up once the microphones are rolling, and it's the host's job to help them open up.

We'll look more closely at the art of interviewing later in this book, but if you are considering an interview or talk-show podcast, you'll want to take these factors into account:

- Interviews give your listeners intimate access to interesting voices and ideas in a familiar format.
- Interviewing a guest takes practice and requires planning and preparation.

- Speaking without an outline or clear direction is a talent that very few have.
- An interview or talk-show style podcast requires less editing and production time when done properly.

Check out: *Museum Archipelago, Museum People, The NYPL Podcast, Art Matters*

Solo Scripted

Solo scripted podcasts usually revolve around a single host who scripts the entire episode. There are some podcasts that use this model for every episode, like *Lore*, but many shows with co-hosts or interviews as their main format use a solo scripted episode occasionally to break things up.

I'm not including solo unscripted shows here because I can't think of a single effective podcast done in this style. It's done, but it's almost never done well. Unless you have a singularly charismatic host or a celebrity that draws listeners in with their star power, you will be hard pressed to create a sustainable solo show without scripting.

You'll learn how to write and read a script later on in the book, but here's the minimum you need to know about solo scripted shows before committing to this format:

- Scripting gives you complete control over the content of the episode.
- Script-writing takes time and research.
- You are not dependent on guests to make the show engaging.

Check Out: *Lore, Revisionist History* (some episodes)

Narrative Radio

Narrative radio shows are often referred to as storytelling podcasts. I don't like that label because every good podcast should tell a story, no matter what style they are. However, narrative radio shows are the ones that really take storytelling to the next level, often using extensive narration and audio from interviews out in the world or in the studio. Music and secondary audio like old news clips enhance the listening experience.

This category includes some of the most well-known podcasts, like *This American Life*, *Radiolab*, *Serial*, and *S-Town*. These kinds of shows are also sometimes referred to as narrative journalism when the medium is being used to uncover stories or discover new facts, like in *Serial*.

If you want to tell historical stories, explore little-known lives, or tell the stories of people in your community, this is a great format to choose.

Narrative radio is unmatched in its non-fiction storytelling potential, but there are a few things to remember before you go this route:

- Collecting audio from multiple sources and being out-in-the field can take time, as can sourcing historical audio.
- The more moving parts you have, the more time will be needed in editing.
- This format allows you to weave multiple sources into one story for a rich listening experience.

Check Out: *Distillations, Texas Story Podcast, Raw Material, Museums in Strange Places*

Audio Drama

Audio drama may not be something you've considered for your institution's podcast. This quickly-growing genre of podcasting is a direct descendant of the radio plays that were popular from the 1930s to the 1960s, updated for modern audiences. Audio dramas are the pure fiction shows of the podcasting world. They tell stories using voice actors, sound effects, and music.

The great ones use the medium of audio to tell stories that couldn't be told any other way, like "broadcasting" from fictional community radio stations (*Welcome to Night Vale* and *King Falls AM*) or telling a story using the audio diaries of a mysterious girl on a spaceship with a voice recorder (*Girl in Space)*. Others use a narrator to drive the story forward in the style of the radio plays of the 1950s (*Distillation*'s episode "Sci-Fi Radio Drama"). Others imitate or parody popular podcast and radio formats, like public radio journalism (*Limetown*) or true-crime investigations (*A Very Fatal Murder*).

Audio dramas can be as simple as one main character with sound effects or as complex as fifty voice actors and a team of sound engineers. By creating a story specifically for audio, you can tell engaging stories with far less cost and manpower than is required for television.

When deciding if an audio drama could set your institution apart, consider this:

- Audio dramas allow for a huge amount of creativity and original storytelling.
- You will need talented amateur or professional actors to make a good audio drama.
- Institutions with a theater component already have lots of talent to draw from.

Who will create the show?

If you are producing a podcast in-house, the interests of the staff members or volunteers who take charge of the project need to be a factor in crafting the show concept. Podcast listeners love to share in a host's passion, so it's important that the creators of the show are excited about the idea and can find the motivation to keep the show going every episode. Additionally, their time commitment to the project and existing skill set may create constraints on what you can do. While you can certainly bring in a host, hire an editor, or get help on any difficult aspects of production, you'll keep the budget lower by working within your existing talents, interests, and skill levels.

Personally, I'm a confident writer and a great conversationalist when the mic is off, but I'm less confident talking off-the-cuff when the mic is on. So I structured my own podcast to be mostly a mix of my interview subject talking and my scripted narration. I'm not saying this to warn you off of trying something challenging or getting out of your comfort zone but to encourage you to play off your strengths or the strengths of those involved in the project. If you are going to be building a team within your organization to work on the podcast together, be open to changing your concept to maximize the existing abilities of your team.

On a practical note, I know that a lot of us in this field are already wearing multiple hats in our roles, so take stock of how many hours a week of staff time are available for this project before you decide to settle on an idea that may require more time investment.

If your organization is committed to creating a great podcast in-house, you may want to build in a budget for hiring a dedicated staff member to help with the podcast or temporarily take over some non-podcasting duties from the podcasting team—either before you begin or conditionally, depending on the podcast's success.

Sustainability

Will your podcast run continually every week for a few years? Will you just produce ten episodes of a single, episodic narrative? Will you batch episodes to create two seasons a year? Will you cover one topic briefly and then move on or give encyclopedic coverage of one specific theme or subject? The scale, longevity, and sustainability of your podcast concept has to be determined before you can create a brand for your podcast.

The Bullock Texas State Museum has a podcast called *Texas Stories*. The first season was completely dedicated to the life and music of Stevie Ray Vaughan. If they had not been planning to continue with a second season on a new topic from Texas history, they would probably have been better off calling it *Stevie Ray Stories*. The same is true for my own podcast, *Museums in Strange Places*. The first year was all about Icelandic museums, and I may have gotten a bit more traction on that subject by naming it accordingly, but I knew I wanted to focus on a different country, state, or region in each season, so I branded the podcast accordingly.

I'll give you more options for batching and production schedules in "Chapter 3: Editing and Production," but for the purposes of refining your concept, you should be able to fill in the blanks in one or both of these sentences (knowing that you can change it later):

Our podcast will have __episodes every [month/year] for __[months/years].

OR

We will work in seasons of approximately __episodes each, taking__ [weeks/months] off between each season. During seasons, episodes will be released every __weeks.

Podcast Idea Inspiration

You've had some time to think through the big planning questions, and I'm guessing you've got at least an initial idea for your podcast. Go ahead and write it down now, even if it's rough.

If you don't have an idea yet, that's okay! No need to worry. Read through the prompts and random ideas below and see what jumps out at you. (I can't promise that these ideas haven't been done before, so if you use one, make sure to do some market research first.)

- Uncover the surprising or untold histories of your town, region, or state.
- Interview members of your community about their personal histories.
- Give lessons on art and art history that children and parents listen to together.
- Hold a "Book club" discussion with a new book each season (The Arlington, Virginia Public Library book club invited their community to read *War and Peace* together over the summer and created the podcast *Oh Boy, Tolstoy!* to offer a discussion space for this online book club).
- Pick one specific topic each season and invite different kinds of people (experts, community members, historians, kids, artists, etc.) to discuss the topic with the host each episode.
- Write an audio drama that takes place in your museum (in the past, present, or future).
- Put on a historical audio drama about the history of your region.
- Create an audio drama about ghosts of artists gathering in your museum every night to discuss art news (*Gossip* is a fictional podcast that lets you listen in on three friends gossiping about the neighborhood).

- Dive into a historic crime from your region in "true crime" style.

- Interview young members of your field about the future of their practice.

- Put local current events in historical context.

- Pick a new topic each season related to your museum or temporary exhibit and interview everyday members of the community about their experiences around it (food, gender, artistic creation, loss, war, etc.)

- Tell the story of an ongoing investigation into a new historical discovery or relevant project in your community (*Serial* did this with true crime, but for cases that were still being decided or debated).

- Collect oral histories or share those in your collection, framing them with historical research and scripted narrative.

- Create an advice show where the advice is specific to your area of focus, or all the advice is what someone would get in, for example, the 18th century (*Dear Sugars* is the best advice podcast out there, offering guidance on all kinds of topics).

- Pick influential living members of your community or field and create audio documentaries about their lives.

- Write an audio drama about the artifacts stored in collections recollecting their lives before they were in a museum. (Remember in *Toy Story 2* when the toys from the toy museum tell their stories?)

- Co-host a talk-show where you cover the latest and greatest in your field or subject matter.

- Produce a how-to podcast offering instruction and answering audience questions, with or without guest experts (gardening, getting involved in your community, having a career as an artist, etc.).

- Make a "travel" podcast that visits the historically significant parts of your town or other locations relevant to your institution.

- Document the making of a large exhibition or program from its conception to take-down.

Thinking Outside the Box

Some of the ideas I just gave you are a little weird. I cannot guarantee all of them would actually work, but I want you to think outside the box. Figure out what is going to set your podcast apart and make potential listeners think, "Now that's something I *have* to hear."

Here's a good rule to keep in mind: the more general your topic, the better your production quality will need to be to pull it off. A good example of how to do a general topic well is *Distillations*, the podcast of the Science History Institute. Each monthly episode takes a deep dive into a different moment of science-related history in order to shed light on the present. The episodes cover a wide variety of subjects within that mandate, like the history of margarine vs. butter, the production of a Ray Bradbury radio play, a biographical piece about a female scientist that history has forgotten, and the ethics of organ transplants.

How are they able to pull this off? Well, *Distillations* may hold the record for the oldest museum podcast; they started releasing episodes in 2008. Over time, they've built up a listener base, so they are able to release only one episode per month and spend the time needed to make it excellent. Each episode has scoring, sound effects, supporting found audio like news clips, excellent scripts, and two great hosts that make every story fun, even when they are discussing a serious topic like acid rain.

Remember, your podcast doesn't have to cover every aspect of your institution. In fact, the more specific you are, the more likely you are to build a devoted listener base. For example, The Jewish Museum & Archives of British Columbia produced *Kitchen Stories*, a limited-run podcast that explored the connections between food, community, and heritage in thirteen episodes.

If your institution is hyper-focused, then don't be afraid to zoom out to address a bigger topic. If you are an archive from a dairy corporation, do a podcast about the role food plays in your community members' lives, and if you have a museum of handbags, create a podcast about women's fashion. If your institution is devoted to the writings of Edgar Allan Poe, create a literary review podcast about contemporary poetry, short stories, or horror.

The unique aspect of your podcast doesn't necessarily have to be the subject matter. It may be a unique take on a familiar topic. *A Piece of Work* by the MoMA explores high-brow contemporary art through refreshingly low-brow conversations between comedian Abbi Jacobson and famous guests. Jacobson takes art forms that many find confusing and uses her conversations with these guests to figure out why these art forms matter. For example, in one episode, she and world-famous drag queen RuPaul sit down to watch video art together. You may not be able to get the stars of pop culture to come on your podcast, but you can still apply the technique of having unexpected guests talk about expected topics.

Long story short, you need to get out of the box and find a uniquely-shaped niche to fill.

Finding Your Voice

Consider the tone of your podcast and how you will engage with the subject matter. Will you offer entertaining history lessons like *Talking Hoosier History* or use your podcast to tackle serious contemporary issues, like the United States Holocaust Memorial Museum's *Voices on Antisemitism*?

It's important to find your podcast's tone. Though *you* may get bored of a serious approach every episode, listeners usually want consistency in this department. Your approach to the subject matter may even be the entire reason they listen.

This is the case for the podcast *Ologies*. In each episode of *Ologies*, host Allie Ward interviews a different "ologist," from linguistic phonologists to volcanologists and everything in between. The subject matter of the show changes dramatically every episode. One week you are learning about rhinology (the study of noses) and the next week you are talking to a curator at The Henry Ford about deltiology (the study of postcards). What keeps me coming back for every episode is the energetic, no-question-too-ridiculous, hilarious host. I know I'll laugh and learn if I start an episode, and even with that familiarity, I'm sure to be surprised by the content.

Of course, this doesn't mean you can't have natural variation within your show! My podcast takes a mostly serious tone, but when the subject matter allows or my interview subject is particularly funny, I may throw in a few jokes. My podcast's unique factor is the format of the show (a new country or region every season, a new museum in that area for every episode), so I have more leeway to let the tone of the museums I visit dictate the tone of each episode.

The WHY

I learned from Jeff Brown, creator of the *Read to Lead* podcast, that listeners want to know the *why* behind your podcast. It will help them know whether or not your show is worth their time. Brown shares his podcast's "why" in the form of a worldview statement.

The worldview statement for *Read to Lead* is this: "I believe that intentional and consistent reading is key to success in business in and in life." Brown even incorporates that statement into his podcast description on Apple Podcasts, which begins, "If you believe as I do, that intentional and consistent reading is key to success in business and in life, then this is your podcast." You can see how that's so much more compelling to potential listeners than "This is a podcast about reading."

Ian Elsner is the host of *Museum Archipelago*, a podcast that explores "the rocky landscape" of the museum field. His worldview is clearly stated in the podcast's description on Apple Podcasts: "Museum Archipelago believes that no museum is an island and museums are not neutral." Before you even start listening, you can decide whether you agree with this statement. If you do agree, you'll listen with the anticipation that you are going to like what the podcast has to say. If you don't, well, you probably wouldn't have kept listening anyway. Every podcast can't be for everyone. Podcasting is all about reaching a niche audience.

Your "why" statement will let listeners know why they should give you a chance, and it will also give them a powerful point of connection with the podcast's message. It's basically a mission statement for your podcast.

You don't have to share it in the form of "We believe *X*," but I recommend trying to incorporate a worldview statement in some way into your podcasting branding and introduction. A mission-led institution needs a podcast with a mission or underlying belief.

Write down the "why" of your podcast now. If you are feeling stuck, use the model of Brown's statement and start with "We believe…"

Now that you are an expert in how to choose a podcast concept, go back and reread the podcast concept you wrote down earlier in this chapter. Does it need to be refined? Is it focused enough? Will listeners know what they can expect to hear?

Rewrite the concept, updating it with the lessons we've discussed in this chapter.

Choosing a Title for Your Podcast

Last, but not least, you need a title for your show! Your title should be short, original, and tell potential listeners what to expect. Here are a few great titles to inspire you:

AirSpace is the podcast of the Smithsonian's National Air and Space Museum. The title is easy to remember, captures the essence of what the museum does, and is a clever wordplay on both airspace and airtime, as in available hours for broadcasting.

GirlSpeak is the podcast of the virtual Girl Museum. The podcast covers "art, history, and contemporary culture from a girl's eye view." It's easy to get that from the title, no explanation needed!

A Piece of Work by the MoMA and WNYC studios explores high-brow art in an unpretentious, humorous manner. The title evokes art, but also has some humor.

Whitest Cube is a show from Palace Shaw and Ariana Lee that investigates "art institutions from the perspective of people of color." The title is original, sticks in your mind, and definitely evokes the "white cube" of elite art institutions while hinting that the hosts are going to be taking a critical approach.

What's Your Elevator Pitch?

Are you familiar with the concept of the elevator pitch? Imagine you find yourself in the elevator with the head of your organization, and they say, "Have you heard that many museums are starting podcasts? Maybe we should have one." You have the rest of the elevator ride to convince them that your idea is worth funding.

You are going to be describing your podcast to a lot of people as you plan, produce, and market your show. It's imperative that you can describe the show and explain why it's unique in 30 seconds or less.

This initial pitch will pique the interest of your listener and open the door to further discussion. On the other hand, if you launch into a five-minute monologue on what's going to be in the show and what's going to be interesting, you will lose your listener and may even give them a negative impression of your idea. Having a great elevator pitch means you are ready at any time to sell someone on the value of your show.

I attend a lot of conferences, and when I meet new people I want to give them an enticing introduction to my podcast and my work in twenty seconds. I need to grab their attention without monopolizing the conversation.

Here's my twenty-second elevator pitch:

> Hi, I'm Hannah Hethmon. I'm a consultant specializing in museum communications, specifically museums and podcasting. My podcast is called *Museums in Strange Places*. It's about exploring the world through its museums. Each season focuses on a different country, state, or region. In each episode, I visit a different museum and discover what stories it holds. You can find it on Apple Podcasts or wherever you get your podcast fix.

Since you are probably going to be pitching your podcast to people who are already familiar with the work of your institution, you'll want to replace the "who am I" section with a statement that highlights the institutional goals you will be meeting through the podcast (use the goals you picked at the beginning of this chapter).

Your elevator pitch should include these elements (in this order):

1. What we do
2. Podcast name
3. Five-second description of the podcast
4. What makes it unique
5. Call to action

Go ahead and write down an elevator pitch for your show based on all the concept refining you've done so far.

Chapter 2
Equipment and Software

If you're like me, researching microphones and other technical equipment is the thing that will make you want to throw something across the room. There are literally hundreds of opinions on the internet about which mics podcasters should use—and most of them are right! So, how do you figure out which setup is right for your needs and budget?

After hours of researching equipment to start my podcast, I became so frustrated that I was on the brink of giving up before I even began. I was saved by Dan Yaeger and Marieke Van Damme of the *Museum People* podcast, who had written a short Technical Leaflet for the American Association for State and Local History (AASLH) on creating a DIY history podcast. They listed the exact equipment they used and the prices. I knew I liked their sound quality, so I decided to just buy the exact same gear. That turned out to be a great decision, and I didn't need to upgrade anything for a year.

Of course, I still had a lot to figure out by myself, but it was such a relief to have someone just *tell* me what to buy. That's what I'm going to do for you in this chapter. If you want to do your own research or want to spend more money on fancier set-ups, go for it. There is no wrong way to record if it sounds good in the end!

The equipment I'm recommending is going to get you a good sound on a budget. You can always upgrade later if you find your setup is not quite meeting your needs. My recommendations are for general needs, so you will have to choose from my several suggestions based on what type of podcast you are doing, and how much time you will need to spend recording in a studio setting or out in the field.

What equipment will you need?

- Microphone(s): One per person in the "studio" or just one handheld if you are interviewing "in the field"
- A handheld recorder
- Windscreens and pop filters for your mics
- Mic stands
- XLR cables
- A pair of studio-grade headphones for recording and editing

Microphone Primer

Let's quickly go over the basic categories of microphones. You can skip this section if you don't care how microphones work. (Really, don't feel bad if you just want to focus on using them at this point. I didn't bother learning most of this until I was doing the research for this book.)

The two main categories of microphones, at least for our purposes, are *condenser* and *dynamic*. Condenser mics are more delicate and sensitive to sound, so you'll typically see these more often in a studio setting where you can eliminate background noise and they don't need to be handled frequently. Dynamic mics are more durable and can be less sensitive to background noise, so these are great for everyday use and field recording.

More importantly, it's nice to know about the *directionality* of your mics. Directionality simply refers to the direction in which the microphone collects sound. *Omnidirectional* mics record in 360 degrees, picking up sound no matter what side of the mic it's on. *Bidirectional* mics record in two opposite directions. *Unidirectional* mics, more often referred to just as *directional* mics, have a more focused zone of recording, recording on the front and sides in a half-sphere shape.

Within directional mics, there are a few sub-categories. *Cardioid* mics pick up noise well in the front and on the sides, but poorly from the back. The name cardioid refers to the heart-shaped zone where the mic picks up sound, but really it's more of a peach shape. If you are in front of the mic, you are at the bottom of the peach, and the crease at the top is where the mic won't pick up much sound. *Hypercardioid* mics pick up noise in a similar shape, but with a narrower width. *Supercardiod* mics have, again, just a narrower zone for recording.

Meet the Zoom H4n Pro Handy Recorder, Your New Best Friend

I am so convinced of the versatility and quality of the Zoom H4n Pro Handy Recorder that I am not going to even list other options for recording. The Zoom family of handy recorders are used by podcasters of every level, and the H4n is one of the most popular. At $200, it's pretty affordable.

The H4n Pro fits comfortably in the hand and can connect to two microphones for easy interviews. There's a short learning curve when you first unbox it, but I'll walk you through the features you need to care about later in this chapter (so you can ignore all the other buttons and settings that may seem overwhelming). You can use it in your "studio" space or in the field (like I usually do), and it's also great for collecting extra sounds to use in your podcast, like the noises of a busy street or birds, if you want to have authentic sound effects.

Some podcasters record directly from microphones to cloud storage or an editing program on their computer. Others use a mixer, which is usually a smaller version of those panels with dials and sliders you'd see in a recording studio. For the sake of flexibility, sound quality, and mobility, I recommend *just* using the H4n as your recorder and not worrying about recording directly to the computer or through a mixer.

Microphone Recommendations

If you read the following section and are still unsure of which microphone you want, go to YouTube and type in a microphone name and "review." There are thousands of people on YouTube who buy and review recording equipment. These reviews will give you a sense of what the mic sounds like. It's especially helpful to watch comparison reviews that contrast the sound of two different microphones. Use your studio-quality headphones when watching these so that you can hear the subtle differences that may be lost coming through your computer speakers.

Audio Technica ATR2100

This is the microphone I used in the first season of my podcast for recording interviews at a table, interviews while walking through museums, and scripted narration in my home. It's very popular among a wide variety of podcasters, simple to use, and can connect to your H4n Pro via an XLR cable or to your computer via USB.

This mic costs $50-65, but you can get a package set on Amazon for $90 that includes a mic stand, pop filter, and TASCAM TH-02 headphones. The headphones cost about $40 if you buy them separately. The mic stand in this package isn't very good, but even if you buy another one for $15, you still come out ahead with the package deal. You'll also want to get a foam windscreen for your mic, which will be about $7.

To hear what this mic sounds like in action, listen to one of the last episodes of *Museums in Strange Places* Season 1, like "The Shark Farm." You can also listen to the podcast *Museum People*, which uses two ATR2100s for everything.

A lot of podcasters start out using the Blue Yeti or Blue Yeti Pro mic to record interviews and scripts in a studio setting. In my opinion, the popularity does not match the quality, and I've heard from a lot of beginner podcasters who struggle to get the sound right and find that they break easily. Many of these people end up switching to the ATR2100.

I think the hype about Blue Yeti is largely the result of more aggressive marketing, the fact that it looks "more professional," and the larger cost that would lead you to believe it is higher quality. The Blue Yeti Pro costs $250, so at $50 the ATR2100, which I think has a better sound, is a much better deal.

Audio Technica AT2020

If you plan to do a lot of narration or solo-scripted parts, the AT2020 is a solid choice for a home-studio set-up. This condenser mic is $100 and will help you get great sounding vocals. Spend a bit extra (around $15) to get a shock mount for this microphone to ensure you don't get any extra noises from vibrations. I recommend only using this as a "studio" mic and using less sensitive mics for recording in the field.

I upgraded to this mic after finishing the first season of my podcast. I had been using the ATR2100 to record my narration, but as my podcasting improved, I realized I had picked all the low-hanging fruit in improving my sound (using the equipment better, creating better sound environments, better speaking techniques, etc.), and upgrading was the only way to take my sound up a notch.

To hear what this mic sounds like in action, check out the audio version of this very book, which I recorded in my home using the AT2020.

MOVO HM-M2 & RØDE Reporter

If you plan to do regular interviews outside a designated recording space, I'd recommend getting a reporter-style mic. The MOVO HM-M2 is $55 and the RØDE Reporter is $130. After using the ATR2100 in the field for a year,

I was getting frustrated by its sensitivity to noises made when I moved my hand on the base of the mic. It's also pretty heavy if you are holding it and moving it between yourself and a guest for an extended period of time.

After a lot of research, I settled on a reporter-style mic for my second season. The RØDE Reporter is a classic, used by journalists and reporters in the field, but it was a bit out of my budget at the time, so I opted for the MOVO HM-M2, which is the same type of mic. I absolutely love this microphone. It's light and portable, with great sound quality, and far less sensitive to handling. If you can afford the RØDE Reporter, it's a great option, but if you want to keep costs down, you won't be disappointed with the MOVO HM-M2.

The downside to these mics is that they are explicitly designed for handheld interviews and presentations, which is achieved with a slight loss in the richness you can get in a studio-like setting.

I used the MOVO HM-M2 to record all but one of my interviews in the field for Season 2 of *Museums in Strange Places*, which will be released in late 2018.

Audio Technica AT8035

The AT8035 is another great option for field recording. It's a *shotgun* mic, so named for looking like a thin shotgun barrel (14" long in this case). Shotgun mics pick up noise fairly narrowly from directly in front of the mic, so they are great for recording in noisier places.

The AT8035 is one of the mics used by the producers of *This American Life*, so if you are doing similar journalistic interviews, this is a good option. You can also hear it in action on a smaller podcast by listening to *Marietta Stories* by Bill Nowicki, a podcast that shares interviews with community members in Marietta, Georgia.

This mic is more expensive than the others I've listed. It's about $270, and you'll also need to buy a foam windscreen ($25) and a pistol grip shock mount

($15-75) to avoid handling noises. Again, if you want to keep costs down for field recording, the MOVO HM-M2 is a great place to start.

Lavalier Microphones

Lavalier mics are those tiny clip-on mics you often see being used in television interviews or reality shows. They usually include three components: the mic itself, the transmitter, and the receiver. The mic clips to a collar or tie, and a small wire connects it to the transmitter box, which is usually clipped on the belt or tucked away somewhere. The transmitter is connected wirelessly (usually over radio frequencies) to the receiver, which can be plugged into a recorder or mixer.

I wouldn't really recommend these for podcasting. I've played around with the Fifine wireless lavalier, but the sound quality just isn't the same, and you end up relying on your guest to not move too much or knock it out of place. They are used more often in scenarios where you need to be hands-free or you are being filmed and a microphone in the way would ruin the shot. However, lavaliers are pretty cheap (starting at $20), so if you want to buy some and experiment, you may find that they fit your particular needs. There are many different brands available to choose from.

Can't We Just Use an iPhone?

These days, it is easy to record audio with smartphones. There are many tutorials showing you how to create a podcast with just your phone. There are even external mics that can fit in your hand and plug into your iPhone jack. Services like Anchor offer apps that let you record straight into your iOS or Android smartphone.

If you are a student making a podcast for fun or an individual who wants to experiment and see if podcasting is right for you, I'd say give it a try. But this book is for podcasts being created within an institution and because of that, there are two big reasons *not* to record on your smartphone.

First, you just won't get the best quality out of a smartphone. Bottom line. And by the time you invest in nice plug-in mics to try and improve the sound, you'll be spending almost as much as you would have for the H4n Pro and ATR2100 combo I recommended.

Second, it doesn't look very professional. If you, as an institution, are going to be interviewing guests and community members, or recording in the field, you don't want those people looking at a mic plugged into an iPhone and thinking you aren't making a professional quality podcast. This may sound vain, but the bottom line is that people are more excited and open to speaking with more established, professional shows.

When I first started, I would struggle to set up my equipment and make apologies for my inexperience with the gear. This did not make a great first impression, and it may even have made some guests less open and engaged than I would have liked. While recording for my second season, I reached out with the message that I was an "international award-winning podcast producer" and showed up with my gear ready to go. It made a difference in how much time and effort my interview subjects were willing to spend helping me get all the tape I needed.

(Side note: *Tape* is the term used in radio and podcasting to refer to your raw audio. It's a leftover term from the days when you were actually recording on tape and editing involved actually cutting tape. I use this term here and there throughout the book, always to refer to the audio you have collected in one way or another.)

Accessories and Extras

What else will you need? If you have the ATR2100, the AT8035, or other similar mics, you'll want to get foam windscreens. This helps prevent those awful noises from wind and *plosives*, the letters and sounds that require you to release a sudden burst of air (like *t*, *k*, and *p*). These range from $5-25, depending on the size.

A pop filter or pop shield will also help keep plosives from sounding too harsh in the recording. If you've ever seen images of singers recording in a studio, the pop filter is the round screen between the singer and the mic. I've found these for as low as $7.

For recording in your "studio," you'll want a stand to keep your mic in the right position. Depending on where you are recording (more on that later), you can get a table-top stand, a suspension boom stand that attaches to shelves and tabletops, or a floor stand so you can record standing up. Depending on what you get, these can be anywhere from $15-30.

You'll also want to get a decent set of studio-grade headphones so that you can hear the nuances in your sound while you are recording and editing. Just using regular headphones won't let you hear as many details clearly, and that will negatively impact your ability to evaluate your recording. These don't have to be expensive though. I use the TASCAM TH-02 headphones that came with my ATR2100 package set, and they work just fine, although you may want to get some with a coiled headphone cable if you plan to be mobile.

Finding a Good Recording Environment

Now that you have all your equipment, it's time to decide where to record. The space where you record is going to have a big impact on your sound quality. If you can call in any favors at institutions with studio space or rent studio space for cheap, it will be worth it. In many cities, there are spaces that provide free or discounted studio space that you may be able to use. It's also worth reaching out to podcast networks and companies with in-house studios, as they may be willing to donate studio-time. However, if you can't find or afford studio-time, don't worry; it's completely possible to get a great sound without a professional studio.

Find a small to medium-sized room in your institution that's quiet. It's much harder to remove unwanted background noise than to just avoid it when recording. Make sure there aren't air conditioning units, noisy appliances, or any fans going that will create strange noises in the background.

You'll want a room that's as dead as possible. In other words: *not* echoey. The echo is going to be one of the biggest things you want to avoid, so look for rooms that are carpeted and have curtains or other things on the walls that will dampen the sound instead of bouncing it back to you. Soft furnishings can help as well.

If you can't find a room that's already ready to use, grab blankets or sheets and throw them over echoey surfaces like table-tops. If you can create a designated spot for recording (like a large closet), you can buy foam soundproofing panels for pretty cheap on Amazon and put those up on the walls to create a studio. Alternatively, if you have someone handy around, you can create panels to set up whenever you record. Creating a triangle recording "booth" of panels or blankets works really well.

You can also buy mobile voice-over booths ready-to-go. Some can be pretty expensive, but you can get a simple sound shield/ isolation shield for around $100. These are just curved panels with acoustic foam that you can set on a table or a stand to isolate your voice from background noise when recording.

When I upgraded to the AT2020 for recording narration and my audiobook, I also purchased a Marantz sound shield, a heavy-duty full-height stand to mount it on, and a laptop stand that clips onto the stand, so I can read my script.

I live in a tiny apartment in Warsaw, Poland with hard floors and tall ceilings and nowhere to set up a permanent recording space, so before I upgraded to the collapsible sound shield, I would open my wardrobe, hang a blanket over the doors, and use a scissor boom arm stand to hold the microphone in front of hanging clothes while recording my scripts. I'm not saying this is a perfect setup, but it did the job, and my sound came out pretty good.

Feel free to get creative. Plug your mic into your recorder, put the monitoring volume all the way up, and speak into the mic in different rooms and setups to figure out what sounds the best. If you are recording in a room with space to move around, find a spot just off the center, away from walls.

Now, if you are recording away from your "studio," there are other factors to consider and you may have less control over your environment. If you are recording indoors at different locations like I often do with my podcast, you may want to walk through the space before you begin and do a quick test to see how the different rooms sound. Once you've done this a few times, you'll be able to judge a room without the testing.

Once you start recording, make sure to have your headphones on the whole time so you can immediately adjust if you realize the room is very echoey or if there's noise from the street outside. Of course, all background noise is not bad. You'll have to evaluate how much ambient noise from the setting you want. For example, if you are recording an episode about a children's program, hearing kids playing and laughing in the background could add a lot to the overall effect.

If you are recording outdoors, again just be aware of the noise levels around you and which sounds you want your audience to hear. Be prepared to stop your subject for a moment if a train starts rumbling or a lawn-mower passes nearby. Also, watch out for wind. When I was recording in Iceland, wind was the single biggest reason for unusable audio. If you *must* record outdoors in a windy location, try to get behind something that will keep the wind from hitting your mic directly or use your body as a windbreak.

Wherever you are recording, pay close attention to how the environment will affect your audio, and test until you get a good sound. Recording is the time when you have the most control over the quality of your audio. Like with photography, it's much harder to fix poor recording choices after the fact, so planning is important.

Setting up the Zoom H4n Pro and the ATR2100

For the sake of simplicity, I'm only going to tell you how to set up and record using the H4n Pro and the ATR2100. If you use a different microphone, the process will be pretty much the same. And if you end up with a different recorder, the settings you need to know will likely be the same, even if the buttons aren't in the same places. The H4n Pro is primarily intended for music recording (like many of the tools podcasters use), so it has a lot of different settings that can be overwhelming when you first open the user manual. As a podcaster, you only need to monitor a few; I'm going to tell you which ones you need to know, and you can ignore the rest. However, I do also recommend reading through the manual, just so you are familiar with all the buttons and any warnings.

Use an XLR cable to plug your microphone into INPUT 1 or INPUT 2 on the bottom of the recorder.

Turn your recorder on using the on/off slider on the left side. If you get a really large SD card, it will take longer to turn on, so I recommend getting a memory card no larger than 16 GB. Make sure the STAMINA mode is off. The switch is located in the battery compartment.

Press the MENU button on the right side. Use the dial above it to find SYSTEM, select it by pressing down on the dial, and then set your date and time.

Press MENU again to get back to the first list and select INPUT. Here are the settings you need to know under INPUT:

LO CUT: This is a filter that helps to eliminate wind or blowing noises. I would leave it off to begin with, but once you are feeling confident with the other features, try one of the first three settings. (Note: Don't get confused by MIC vs. INPUT. The H4n has a built-in mic, so where you see MIC on the H4n, it refers to this one, not your plugged-in microphone.)

MONO vs. STEREO: This dichotomy will come up a lot in recording audio. Mono is when all the sound sources are routed through one audio channel. If you are listening to mono in headphones, it will be exactly the same in each ear. Podcasts are almost always in mono or joint stereo, which is effectively like mono. Stereo reproduces multiple sources, allowing you to experience a more natural distribution of musical components between two earbuds, for example.

1/2 LINK and MONO MIX: 1/2 LINK turns on automatically when MONO MIX is on. MONO MIX records all mics attached to the H4n into one track. 1/2 LINK connects the two inputs on your recorder. If you are only recording with one microphone, you need to have these settings on. Otherwise, you will end up with an audio track that mysteriously only plays on one side of your headphones. If you are recording with two microphones, you have two options. First, you can record in the same settings, ending up with one track that has the sound from both mics. Or, you can turn MONO MIX and 1/2 LINK off, which will leave you with a separate track for each of your microphones. This will allow you to edit them separately and then mix back down to mono or joint stereo when you publish.

PHANTOM POWER: You will only need this to be on if your microphone requires it. Just look at the user manual for your microphone to find out if you need phantom power. The

ATR2100 and MOVO HM-M2 do not need phantom power. The AT8035 does. Keep in mind that your batteries will run out faster if you are using phantom power.

Now confirm that you are recording in stereo by checking the three lights at the top of the recorder. (Confused because I said to record in mono? You *are* recording on the STEREO setting, but the MONO MIX setting will convert the track to mono.) As a podcaster, you don't need to worry about the other two settings, 4CH and MTR. If the light is not on above STEREO, go to the menu and select MODE. Then select STEREO.

Last, check the input buttons on the left front panel; 1 and 2 should have lights next to them and MIC should be off. This is how you know that the H4n Pro is recording from your plugged-in external microphone and not the internal microphone.

OK! You are ready to record. Plug your headphones into the jack on the left side of the recorder and press the REC button once to start recording standby. The light should blink. This will allow you to hear what the mic sounds like without actually recording.

If you can't hear anything, check the headset volume on the left side of the recorder. Note that this volume button *only* changes the volume in your headphones. It does not affect the volume at which you are recording. To change the recording volume, adjust the REC LEVEL on the right side of your recorder.

Try starting your levels (REC LEVEL) on 80, then adjusting down if there's too much background noise being picked up. Test out a few different levels, speaking the adjustments you are making into the mic as you go. Then you can listen back to the test audio, hearing the difference.

Once you are happy with your levels, press REC once more, and you will see the counter start on the screen. This is how you know you are actually recording. If the counter isn't advancing, you are not recording! You can pause and restart your recording with the play/pause button on the front panel. When you are ready to end this recording session, press the stop button.

To see your recording, go to the menu and select FILE. You should see your most recent recording at the top. Use the dial above MENU to scroll to your file and press it to select. Once you have selected your file, you will be returned to the main recording screen, except you will see your file name displayed under the counter. Press the play button and you'll be able to hear the recording you just made (only with headphones plugged in).

To access your recordings, remove the SD card, insert it into your computer, and copy the files into a new folder. I like to leave the original recording on the SD card until the episode is finished and online just in case something crashes on my computer. I also backup all my recordings with cloud storage, something I strongly recommend (I use Google Drive), especially because they can take up a lot of space in your computer's storage.

Congratulations, you now know everything you need to record using a Zoom H4n Pro!

Using the Microphone

The microphone is primarily recording what is in front of it—depending on the type of mic it will pick up more or less from the sides. The closer your voice is to the microphone, the more voice you'll get and the less background noise you will get. Closer to the mic, you will get more bass and a richer sound; farther from the mic, your voice will be thinner.

Some people are naturally louder or project more, so you will have to adjust how close the speaker is depending on their volume. If you are getting a lot of harsh *sibilants* (the hissing noises from *s* and *z*), move the microphone slightly to the left or right so you are not speaking directly into it.

The best placement of the microphone in relation to your mouth depends on the type of microphone and the speaker, but four inches away is a good place to start. Experiment with placing the microphone a few inches away at lip height, pointing down from a few inches above the lips, and pointing up from a few inches below the lips. Test with each person who will be regularly speaking on your podcast and make some notes about what works best.

There are endless tutorials for speaking into a mic online, but I recommend just experimenting and recording some test tracks to figure out what sounds best to you with your mic in your space.

If you are recording in your "studio" space, make sure your mic is on a stable stand. Some noise from handling can occur when you are doing interviews in the field, but you can avoid this during stationary interviews.

For an in-person, face-to-face interview, use two dynamic mics like the ATR2100 and make sure they are in stands facing opposite directions. Remember that they will record to the front and sides. Do a 10-minute test-run interview with somebody before you try this with your first real guest.

For an interview, you can also sit close to your guest and both speak into the same directional mic. I have done this a number of times with the ATR2100, and if the room sound is good, it works just fine. You just have to get really cozy with them; try sitting on either side of a table corner with your knees almost touching, both turned slightly towards the mic so that you, your guest, and the mic make a triangle.

Recording Remotely

Not every guest you want to interview will be able to travel to your institution to record. The best way to record remotely is to use a virtual meeting or call software that allows you to record calls. Many podcasters do interviews through Skype, using software to record the calls. Zencaster is an online platform specifically designed for remote podcast interviews. Zoom is another platform that many podcasters use to do remote interviews.

There are also a number of apps for phones that will let you record phone calls. I highly recommend testing out different methods before you ever call up a guest. Speaking from experience, you don't want to do a whole interview on Skype, only to realize that the recording is unusable.

What to Record?

In this chapter, I've covered the *how* of recording, but not the *what*. We're going to move on to editing and production next, but I will come back to interviewing and recording in "Chapter 4: Storytelling for Podcasters."

Chapter 3
Editing and Production

Editing is one of my favorite parts of podcasting. It's when everything you've gathered comes together and—with some hard work—transforms into a story that your listeners will enjoy. In this chapter, I will show you how to use free software to edit your audio.

Audacity is a free open-source digital audio editor and recording application software. You may have a short learning curve with Audacity, but once you get the hang of it, you'll find it well-suited to editing any kind of podcast. To get it on your computer, just go to https://audacityteam.org and download the version for PC or Mac.

Some beginner podcasters use Garageband, a software that comes pre-installed on Apple computers; more advanced podcasters will often purchase software like Adobe Audition. Garageband is fine but doesn't have all the features you can find in Audacity. Audition is more difficult to master, and I doubt you will need any of its additional features that aren't provided by Audacity.

Audacity is one of the best options for editing podcasts. It's free, and because it's open-source, there is a large online community actively creating tutorials and instructional videos. You can find the Audacity Manual—a website of tutorials and articles on every Audacity function—at https://manual.audacityteam.org/. There are also tons of Audacity tutorials available on YouTube.

Need-to-Know Functions in Audacity

To get started, open up Audacity and use File>Import>Audio to add all your audio files for the episode into one "Project File." Each recording will appear as a separate track, one below the other.

You can use the tab next to the file name on the left end of each track to change its name, making it easier to keeps tabs on what you have.

Using the zoom buttons on the toolbar, you can expand your track to a level that is convenient for editing.

There are lots of functions and tools available in Audacity, but as a podcaster, you really only need to worry about a few:

Cut/Paste: Using the I-shaped Selection Tool, you can select audio, cut, and paste just like you would in a word document, using your keyboard shortcuts or the functions under Edit in the menu.

Clip Boundaries: Under Edit>Clip Boundaries, you will find the Split and Join functions. Split will separate your audio into individual sections within a single track at whatever point you have selected with the Selection Tool. This allows you to differentiate between different segments of one audio track.

Time Shift Tool: Use this horizontal arrow to move segments of your track forward and back and create spaces between them.

Amplify: This is how you raise or lower the volume on your audio. Just select the section you want to adjust, and then choose Effect>Amplify. Begin by adjusting audio in increments of 4 or 5. Note that past a certain point (depending on your track), you will not be able to apply the effect without selecting "Allow Clipping." Do not allow clipping. Only amplify as much as you can without it, otherwise, you will damage your audio. You can see the relative volumes of your tracks by their height and the scale on the left side of the track.

Fade in/Fade Out: Just what it sounds like, the Fade In and Fade Out functions taper your audio in or out. Select the section you want to fade and find this function under Effect on the menu.

Envelope Tool: The Envelope Tool, located near the Selection Tool and Time Shift Tool, is like a more versatile Fade In/Fade Out. It allows you to adjust the volume of your track by drawing a line up and down to control the relative volume. I use this for bringing music up and down as needed for scoring. I rarely use it on my main audio, as Amplify is better for adjusting the volume in small sections.

Sync-Lock Tracks: Under Tracks, you will see Sync-Lock Tracks. If you select this, it will lock all your tracks together, so they move as one.

Save as vs. Export: When you choose Save As, you will save as an Audacity Project File. This is how you should save a work in progress. When you are finished, you will need to choose File>Export and export your episode as an MP3. The default setting is Joint Stereo. You can leave it there or select Force Export to Mono. I won't go into details, but the end result is basically the same. I export in the default Joint Stereo.

Auponic vs. Sound Engineering

You may have noticed that I left out the Audacity functions for engineering sound. There are a number of different ways you can use Audacity to engineer a better sound from your raw audio, and this is where things can get a little complicated and some people (me) might get frustrated trying to compare ten different sets of instructions from the internet.

I wasted hours on each of my first dozen episodes trying to perfect my sound and going down rabbit holes of online tutorials—that is, until I found Auphonic.

Auphonic is an online and desktop application that automatically analyzes and processes your audio to its best possible sound. It will balance your levels, normalize loudness, and restore audio with noise and hum reduction and filtering of unwanted low frequencies.

I cannot recommend this service enough, and you can use it to process two hours of audio for free every month or pay just a few dollars to purchase additional processing time. Simply upload your audio file, ignore all the options except Output Files, the final section at the bottom (choose WAV 16-bit PCM under Format).

Make sure all the boxes are checked, including Noise and Hum Reduction (the reduction amount should be on Auto). Use the drop-down menu under Loudness Target to select -16 LUFS (Podcasts and Mobile) and then Start Production. You'll be able to download your finished audio as a WAV file, ready to be edited in Audacity.

Editing in Audacity

In the following sections, I'll be sharing my own process for editing. Please keep in mind that I edit my episodes very heavily, so my process is longer and more complicated than you may need. I want to give as much detail as possible for those that want to try more complicated episode structures, but I encourage you to adjust and adapt these methods to your own needs.

Once I've cleaned up my audio in Auphonic, I use Audacity for two types of edits: major edits and minor edits. My major edits involve cutting out sections of the conversation that are unimportant to my narrative and re-arranging parts of the conversation so that they fall into "chapters" or logical sections.

The extent to which you need these kinds of edits will depend on the type of podcast you are producing, the quality of your tape, and the amount of time you can commit to the episode. A thirty-minute interview show with a guest who stays on topic (or a host that keeps them focused) will need far less editing than a narrative radio show that uses three hours of tape and scripting to create a twenty-minute story.

So, if you know you can only spend two hours editing an episode, you need to gather tape accordingly, keeping your interviews short and focused and your story simple so that it doesn't need ten separate scripted sections woven into the interview or other audio.

Minor edits are more about sound quality and the listenability of your audio. These are things like cutting out excessive *ums*, shortening long pauses, and taking out noises and your subject's vocal tics. For example, Icelanders tend to make sharp inhalations before starting a new sentence, so when I was editing interviews about Icelandic museums, I'd try to take some of those out, as they didn't translate well to the clean sound I like to achieve in my episode.

The challenge when making minor edits is to preserve the natural sound of your subject's voices while removing noises that are distracting. This is something that takes practice but err on the side of removing less when you are beginning so that you aren't making your subjects voices sound choppy or unnatural.

Again, the extent to which you make these kinds of edits will depend on the quality of your recording and how much time you have to dedicate to it. I like to do this type of fine-combed editing after I have already done my major edits and have my story in the right order with scripting and music roughly in place. This prevents me from getting distracted by *ums* when I need to be focused on telling a good story.

Organizing the Story

It can be difficult to organize your various audio files and keep track of segments when you are editing. Unlike when editing video, you aren't able to quickly scroll through and look for the scene you want. That is why it is very important to have a system for doing your major edits and building your story.

A great place to start is *logging your tape*. This is the process of loosely transcribing your audio so that you can visualize the story. You shouldn't spend too much time on this process; just transcribe into a word document as the file plays without stopping, trying to focus on capturing the beginning and end of segments as well as the important ideas and moments you'll need to make editorial decisions.

Don't worry about spelling, proper punctuation, or any polishing. This is just a visual reference to help you organize your tape. I like to listen to my audio once through before logging it, cutting out any obviously useless segments and using clip boundaries to split the audio into logical sections based on theme or topic as I go. Then I go through again, logging the tape in paragraphs that correspond to the audio segments, making sure I get the first and last words in each segment, so they are easy to find again.

Once I have all my audio segments in front of me in a word document, I can look over it, identifying themes and thinking about the order I want to present it in. While I don't always follow this rule, I try to identify an introduction, several body topics, and a conclusion; it can help to literally add section headers in bold to make this concept more concrete.

As I look over the document, I often start making notes for my script in italics between paragraphs. (The italics differentiate between script notes and tape log.) If I spot any sentences that need to be cut, I will underline them, so I know to cut them out of the audio later.

This is also how I mark audio that I need for the story, but for whatever reason cannot be used. I'll put a note above the paragraph to include that idea or element of the story in my script instead. This is something I had to do a lot in an episode where my subject spoke quickly with a heavy accent, and some audio I normally would have used had to be cut because it was too difficult to understand. I personally like to log my tape and work on these tasks in Google Docs, where it's easy to leave big comments on the side about what needs to be done with each section.

I will then rearrange the paragraphs—if needed—to change the order the audio plays, making sure not to split paragraphs on the document without making the same change to the audio. Once I have a rough order that I like, I rearrange the audio segments in my Audacity project file to match the log, which has now turned into an *episode map*.

Building the Episode

Once I have my story in the right order, I can begin to write my script around the audio segments. For this stage, I like to keep my document and Audacity project open side by side so I can listen, write, listen, write. It's important to make sure to your script naturally flows into the audio segments (and vice versa). Listening to the audio before and after writing a piece of script also helps you find the right tone and timing for your writing.

Remember to write the way you speak. The way you structure a sentence might be very different from an article to audio. For example, the following sentence is something I might write in an article or blog post:

> *According to Rakel, one of the archive's primary goals was to achieve the broadest representation of Icelandic women as possible...*

But when I was writing about this subject for a script, I had to think about how I would have told a friend about the same subject in a conversation:

> *Rakel told me that one of the main goals of the archive was to have a broad representation of women in Iceland...*

And if I am using this bit of script to introduce a segment of audio from my interview with Rakel, I would usually write it in the present tense so that I am narrating the story, not recounting it:

> *Rakel tells me that one of the archive's main goals is to have a broad representation of women in Iceland...*

The best way to make sure that you write like you speak is to read your script aloud as you write it. Read the final version out loud to a friend or colleague who can tell you if any lines sound awkward. If you are more confident in your speaking skills than your writing abilities, you can always speak your script into the mic, transcribe, edit, and then re-record.

You'll find two examples of my scripts in the *Worksheet and Template Bundle*. Here are some additional tips to improve your script-writing:

- Use simple vocabulary, avoiding fancy literary words. For example, use "opposite" rather than "antithesis" or "stubborn" rather than "obstinate."

- Consider the order of your sentence. Start with the information you listener needs to know before providing details; otherwise, they might get confused trying to figure out what you are referencing.

- Don't worry about proper grammar when writing your script. End sentences in prepositions, use fragments, and make pauses with ellipses instead of trying to find the right formal punctuation to convey that pause. We don't speak with proper punctuation or follow every rule of grammar when speaking, so it's not necessary for your script.

Use the same techniques to record your script that I laid out in the chapter on recording your interviews.

Recording your script can be challenging at first, but the more you practice, the more natural it will become. If you've taken the advice above and written your script like you speak, then you will have a much easier time. Make sure to read your script aloud at least once or twice before you hit record, making sure to pause and breathe at natural points like commas and periods.

If you are struggling with speaking naturally, print out your script and use highlighters to give yourself visual cues on where to pause, where to go slowly, and so on. You can also try reading the script in a few funny voices or accents in order to get out of your own head.

Once you have your tape organized, your script recorded, and an outline or episode map, it's time to put it all together and polish any rough parts.

My process is to create three tracks in one Audacity project: the edited audio segments, the recorded script, and a new blank track where you can assemble everything. Using my episode map, I will carefully cut and paste everything into the right order. At this point, I don't worry too much about distances between audio segments, since I still need to add music and sound effects.

During the editing and scriptwriting process, I write notes in the episode map for where music and sound effects should go, and I usually add them to the Audacity file as the last step.

Once everything is in the right order, I go back through once more to make sure everything is lined up properly without awkward gaps and make any necessary minor edits I missed.

How Long Should the Episode Be?

This is one of the most common questions I get from folks interested in starting a podcast for their institution or as a personal hobby. I hate to give you a non-answer, but there is no universal "right" length. Podcast episodes can range from five minutes to two hours long.

The really important thing to monitor is not how long your episodes are, but how interesting they are. How long will people listen before they get bored? If you can keep your listeners engaged and entertained for two hours, then you can do two-hour-long podcasts. That said, twenty to forty minutes is a common podcast length.

You don't have to stick to one strict length. There's no time slot you have to fit in, so one episode might be twenty-two minutes, and another might be twenty-six. That said, it's best to keep them around roughly the same length—at least at first—so that your listeners know what to expect.

If you find yourself ending up with episodes that are forty minutes or longer simply because your interview material is that long, stop and ask yourself, "Do my listeners really *need* to hear all of this?" Cutting down your tape to its best possible length can be extremely difficult; it's easy to become emotionally invested in every part of the interview.

But, as with a history exhibit at a museum, it's not your job to convert a peer-reviewed monograph into wall text or audio. Your job is to inspire, entertain, and inform the public. If you are struggling to keep your episodes under an hour, try recording less. Conduct shorter interviews, write shorter scripts, and so on: have a rough episode length in mind from the early planning stages.

I often tell institutions that are starting out to aim for twenty-minute episodes. It's easier to avoid long, boring sections in a shorter podcast, and of course the shorter the episode, the less time is typically needed to edit.

Using Music and Sound Effects in the Introduction

Music and sound effects can be extremely useful in setting the mood for your podcast and telling a more engaging story. They can also easily become a distraction from the main content, so for most beginner podcasters, I recommend using them in moderation.

In this section, you will learn best practices for using music and sound effects in your podcast. Then we will address legal issues to be aware of when choosing music and where to find free or cheap music.

Music is commonly used in introductions and to create a break in the middle of the episode or between two separate scenes or topics. Let's look at introductions first. Think about some of your favorite TV shows; just a few seconds of theme music can immediately grab you and get you excited for the episode. When I hear "Lock the Gates!" and the familiar guitar riff that kicks off every episode of *WTF with Marc Maron*, I smile to myself, knowing I'm about to enjoy an hour of entertainment. A carefully-selected clip of music for your podcast introduction will do the same for your listeners.

Listen to other podcast intros to get a feel for what sounds good. A starting timeline is this: begin with a few seconds of music, fade the music down, have 10-15 seconds of introduction, and then fade back up for another 15-20 seconds of music (at most).

To do this, add your music as a new track to your Audacity project (so that it's underneath the main audio). Then use the Envelope Tool to fade the music in and out. Use the Fade In/Fade Out effect just for the very ends of the audio to make the transitions as smooth as possible.

You'll notice that I recommend using just a very short piece of music for your introduction. In television, you'll often see longer theme montages, but in audio, you don't have video to keep your audience's attention while the music plays, so you need to keep it short and sweet, getting into the episode content sooner rather than later.

Now, if you've listened to my podcast, you know I don't follow this rule for keeping music short. In almost every episode, I use a different original song from the country, state, or region I am highlighting that season. Music in my podcast is an important part of the journey of cultural immersion and exploration I'm attempting to give to my listeners. Because I put so much effort into picking great songs that change each episode, I will sometimes play up to 45 seconds *after* my introductory lines.

However, most podcasters who use music in their introduction use the same tune every time, so unless you are doing something like my approach in your episodes, I'd recommend keeping the intro music short and sweet—just something to let your listeners know it's time for their favorite podcast.

Other instances when I extend my introductory music longer are in episodes where I have scripted a dramatic opening. For example, in "The Art of Volcanoes," I open with a quote from *Journey to the Center of the Earth* and then go on to describe the majesty of a mighty Icelandic volcano capped with a massive glacier. I wanted my listeners to feel the awe and wonder that comes from seeing this volcano in real life. My score for this episode was a stirring instrumental piece, and I used about two minutes of it under the opening quote, my intro lines, and my scripted preface. To keep it from overwhelming the narrative, I used the Envelope Tool to bring the music volume up and down as needed to emphasize dramatic pauses and enhance my script.

One last thing to keep in mind when using music in your intro: relative volume. You don't want to drown out your voice or suddenly blast your audience's ears through their headphones. The music also needs to be loud enough that it can be heard clearly on a variety of speakers; otherwise, it could end up as an irritating jumble in the background. As you are learning how to use music in your podcast, make sure to listen to your finished episodes on several different devices (headphones, speakers, in the car, etc.) before publishing, so you have a good feel for how it sounds "in real life."

You don't have to use intro music. In fact, you don't have to use music at all in your episodes. Instead, your introduction may have a familiar few lines or a routine that get people hooked. A great example of this is the podcast *Ologies*. One of the biggest draws of *Ologies* is the weird, quirky, hilarious host, Allie Ward. And in keeping with the overall tone of the podcast and the general silliness it brings to the table, she starts every episode off with a variation on the same off-kilter introduction before telling her listeners what kind of "ologist" she is interviewing in that particular episode. There's no music in the first few minutes, just funny references and word-play:

"Oh hey, hey it's the lady from your mom's book club, the one who apologizes even when she brings cookies. Yeah, hi, it's Allie Ward, back with another episode of *Ologies*."

"Oh hey, it's your uncle's corduroy jacket that smells like pipe smoke and breakfast sausages. Allie Ward, back with another episode of *Ologies*."

"Oh hey-lo. It's that lady that sells air plants in abalone shells at the farmers' market. Allie Ward. Back with another episode of *Ologies*."

Ologies does have a little bit of theme music, but it plays a few minutes into the podcast to signal to the listener that the episode is reaching the core content (the interview).

Using Music and Sound Effects in the Episode

Don't use music just because you think you should. As I just explained, you can make a great podcast without any music or sound effects. Music should enhance the story in your podcast, drive the episode forward, and make the show more entertaining. If your music is distracting from your narrative or making it difficult to pay attention to whomever is speaking, then it's detracting from your podcast instead of enhancing it.

Don't feel like you need to add a score to your entire episode. If you want to include some music, it's perfectly acceptable to have some in the introduction, at the end, and serving as a few moments of transition between major segments in the episode. These moments of transition can give the listener a quick break, re-focus their attention, and break up monotonous sections.

The best advice I've found on sound designing/soundscaping in podcasting comes from Rob Rosenthal at Transom, an offshoot of American Public Media dedicated to training folks in best practices for public media. In "Avoiding Cheesy Sound Design," Rosenthal distills advice from the best sound designers in the public radio field into these four steps:[3]

1. Begin by asking why. Why does a segment of a story need sound design? What problem are you trying to solve? What value will it bring?
2. Be ethical. Produce in a way that doesn't trick a listener into thinking what they're hearing is real.
3. Avoid literal sounds. Try mood boarding, an approach to brainstorming that fosters abstract thinking.
4. Iteration. Produce and listen, produce and listen, produce and listen… always with others, until you get it right.

My advice to you is to start small. Try using a bit of music or sound effects in the episode and see how it sounds. As you get more confident in using sound design more effectively, experiment with more elements. Testing out music and sound effects can quickly eat up hours of time, so set yourself a timer for how long you will work on this aspect of the episode, and then get back to the core content. If your story is not engaging, then no amount of sound design will fix that.

---

[3] Rosenthal, Rob. "Avoiding Cheesy Sound Design." *Transom*. November 28, 2017. https://transom.org/2017/avoiding-cheesy-sound-design/.

Where to Find Music?

Now that you know how to use music and sound effects in your podcast, the big question is where to find the right tracks and sounds. Before we go into that, I want to make it clear that you should always have written permission before using any music or sound effects. Sometimes that permission may be built into the website or software you are using to source clips, but if not, you will need to get it directly from the artist or whoever else has the authority to make that decision.

(Note that I am not a legal expert, and no part of this book should be taken as legal advice. Please consult a legal expert if you are unsure of how copyright laws apply to your show.)

You *cannot* just find a song on the internet or iTunes and put it in your podcast. Unless it is already in the Public Domain, this would be considered in most cases a copyright violation. Many beginner podcasters will ask about Fair Use, which is a doctrine of law in the U.S. that allows limited use of copyrighted materials if they are discussing the material directly. This means you *may* be able to use a clip of a TV show or song if you are reviewing it or otherwise speaking directly about it.

However, the rules for Fair Use are not cut and dry, and this is not intended as a loophole for creators who just want to use copyrighted materials without a license. Please err on the side of not using any copyrighted materials for which you cannot get explicit permission to use and consult a legal expert before including any such materials in your show.

Now, that may sound intimidating, but the good news is that there are many ways to find incredible music, sound effects, and supporting audio clips for your podcast without infringing on any copyrights:

The Free Music Archive (http://freemusicarchive.org): This website holds an "interactive library of high-quality, legal audio downloads." Their music is "pre-cleared for certain types of uses that would otherwise be prohibited by copyright laws that were not designed for the digital era." Some songs on T*he Free Music Archive* are already in the Public Domain, which means you can just use them freely. However, others have varying levels of protections under Creative Commons licenses. There is a "License Guide" on the website that will help you know when you need to contact artists and ask permission as well as how and when to credit them in your episode.

Freesound (http://freesound.org): This is a "huge collaborative database of audio snippets, samples, recordings, and bleeps" that have been released under Creative Commons licenses that allow their reuse. I use *Freesound* to find noises of wildlife, boats, cars, doors closing, volcanoes erupting, or other noises I need to soundscape my podcast and bring a scene to life. Again, just make sure to check the Creative Common license on each sound and properly credit the creators.

Soundly (http://getsoundly.com): *Soundly* is a sound effects platform that you can download to your Mac or PC. It offers a great selection of free ambient noise and sound effects that you can use without any copyright restrictions. You can also subscribe for a wider selection.

PodSound (http://podsound.com): Designed specifically for podcasters, *PodSound* is an online subscription service that offers more downloads of royalty-free music per month than you could possibly need. The fees are pretty low, and the selection is great. The service is newer, and the website can be a bit cumbersome to use, but I've found the support staff responsive and helpful.

Local Bands: This is my favorite way to get great music. In the past, most music was released on a label, but today more bands are releasing their music directly without waiting to be picked up by a record label. Many of these bands are excited to have their music in podcasts. They may ask for a one-time fee for use, depending on how many times you plan to use the song in question. It's always best to pay artists for their work if you can. This is also a great way for you to connect with local musicians and highlight artists in your own community. If you go this route, make sure to give clear credit to the artists in the episode, episode description, show notes, and wherever else you can.

Original Compositions: If you want bespoke music that you can use without any limitations, consider hiring a local musician to compose a few tracks for your podcast. Since you are commissioning the songs, you will get documentation that says they are yours to use as you see fit without any restrictions.

Wikimedia Commons: There is lots of historical video on *Wikimedia Commons* that you use without restrictions. Other online archives offer historical videos in the public domain searchable by topic and date as well. Just convert these mp4s to mp3s so you can use them in your podcast.

Check Your Work!

It can be tempting to just export your finished file and put it straight online. You've already spent so many hours on it, and you probably don't want to hear your own voice one more time. But you must proof-listen to your episode carefully, checking for pauses that are too long, missing musical elements, and who knows what else!

I also recommend that, while you are learning, you have a friend, colleague, or family member who was not involved in the process listen to the finished episode and offer a critique. Ask them to answer a few key questions: Is it too long? Did you get bored anywhere? What did you think of the music? What was your favorite part? This also helps with self-doubt and imposter syndrome, which are hard to avoid in any creative endeavor.

Streamlining Your Production Process

I've given you a look at my process for producing each episode. Once you've tried one or two episodes, you should write down a checklist for your own process. As you make changes to this workflow, update the checklist. Having it on-hand while you work will ensure you don't skip any of the effective methods you've added to your production process.

Here's my checklist, which I am constantly updating. Use it to model your own, or create one from scratch. I don't have any deadlines on mine here, but it can be helpful to add them in to help yourself keep things moving quickly. In the *Worksheets and Templates Bundle*, you'll find a *Production Process Checklist* that you can customize.

The Interview

1. Choose the interview subject/museum.
2. Schedule the interview.
3. Prepare for the interview with online research.
4. Before beginning the interview, ask the interview subject to give me a 15-minute tour of the museum.
5. Mentally map out how the interview will go.
6. Conduct the interview.

Editing & Production

1. Run the raw interview audio through Auphonic.
2. Listen to the whole interview in Audacity, cutting unwanted sections and dividing the audio into thematic sections as I go.
3. Log the tape, focusing on opening/closing lines and key sentences.
4. Using the log, organize the story, turning it into an episode map.
5. Write the script around the log, underlining sections that should be cut.
6. Record the script.
7. Run the raw script audio through Auphonic.
8. Add the script audio to the Audacity project.
9. Edit the script and cut it into sections corresponding to the episode map.
10. Add music and sound-effect files to the Audacity file.
11. Assemble the episode using the episode map as a reference. Make minor edits as needed.
12. Listen back through the episode in Audacity, fixing any mistakes and making any necessary minor edits.
13. Export the finished episode and listen with regular headphones like earbuds to check sound, volume, and accuracy. Spot check on speakers or car stereo if possible.
14. Correct any mistakes then re-export.

Publishing & Marketing

1. Write the episode description and title, including any necessary credits.
2. Upload the episode to Libsyn and schedule.
3. Create a show-notes page and schedule it to release at the same time as the episode.
4. Promote the released episode on Twitter, Facebook, Instagram, and LinkedIn.

5. Send the episode directly to anyone who might find a particular interest in this episode's subject.
6. Write any agreed-upon articles for outside websites and blogs.

Save Time by Batching Episodes

One way to save time and prevent this podcast project from taking over your work week is to batch episodes. Batching is just the practice of finishing multiple episodes before you begin releasing.

It's common practice to batch a few episodes before you launch your podcast. This gives you some breathing room to tackle the next episodes without running into unforeseen delays that can easily occur when you are a beginner to podcasting.

Batching is a useful practice to keep up after launch as well. Many podcasters try to keep three or four episodes ready to go at all times so that they don't have to scramble to finish another episode or miss one if something comes up. It's important that your podcast comes out consistently, whether you release once a week or once a month.

For busy museum and history professionals, also consider batching your whole season. By concentrating the work into one period of time, you can create up to half a year's worth of episodes all at once, and then you only have to work on marketing them as they release. This method can also justify the hiring of a temporary assistant or intern to help produce the season over a shorter period of time.

Chapter 4
Storytelling for Podcasters

We've covered a lot of practical lessons so far, but now it's time to turn our attention to the less tangible elements that distinguish great podcasts from "meh" podcasts. These pretty much all fall into the category of *storytelling*.

At this point, a few of you may have thought, "Wait, we're doing an interview podcast, so we aren't telling a story." I'm here to politely but firmly tell you that 99% of podcasts need a story. What do I mean by story? I mean a story by the simplest of definitions: a description of people and events, which is written or told in order to entertain or inform.

Have you heard of the Three-Act Structure? Often credited to Aristotle, it's the format almost every story you encounter will follow—from a Hollywood blockbuster to a great joke told by an indie comic in your local comedy club.

The First Act: This is where you set the stage (also called "exposition"). It's where you introduce the characters and the place or the historical context for an event or movement. It's also where you introduce the conflict, the first problem or challenge; remember discussing man vs. nature or man vs. man in freshman English classes?

Let's say that you are telling the story of a famous female artist, X, who is immensely talented. In the first act, you introduce your listeners to X and share her background and current surroundings (historical, physical, etc.). Then she encounters conflict. There has to be something that alters or disrupts the facts about her life. Otherwise, you aren't telling a story; you are sharing facts.

In this case, maybe the prestigious art academy won't accept female painters. No one wants to hear a podcast about how "X was very talented, she sold some paintings, and her life went as expected without any incidents." The first act might also introduce a question: "Will X overcome the patriarchy and take her rightful place in the art world?"

The Second Act: Now that you've introduced the conflict, it needs to play out. How does X try to get into the academy? Does she enlist other members of the art elite? Does she bring a lawsuit? Does her single-minded pursuit of this goal cause her personal relationships to deteriorate?

The Third Act: Once you have set up the story and your listener is invested in what happens, you need to resolve the story. Does X break through and end up running the academy one day? Or does the struggle leave her in bad health, resulting in her death and her art going unrecognized for the next few decades?

Stories activate the listener's brain in ways that straightforward fact delivery simply can't.[4] Stories about food activate the sensory cortex. Stories about movement and action spark our motor cortex. When a storyteller is connecting to their audience, they can share experiences, not just facts; the parts of the storyteller's brain that light up when they are telling one part of the story will also light up in the listeners' brains.

So, if you want your listeners simply to know that X the artist lived and struggled, you might share some facts. But if you want your listeners to viscerally understand the rejection that X the artist felt and the injustice of women's oppression in the past, then you have to tell a story.

---

[4] Widrich, Leo. "The Science of Storytelling: Why Telling a Story Is the Most Powerful Way to Activate Our Brains." Lifehacker. June 24, 2013.https://lifehacker.com/5965703/the-science-of-storytelling-why-telling-a-story-is-the-most-powerful-way-to-activate-our-brains.

Likewise, if you are interviewing a guest, and you want your listeners to know that they made an amazing historical discovery, you could just ask them to tell you what they found. But if you want your listeners to truly feel the significance of this new research, you need to ask your guests questions that reveal the story of how they came to this conclusion and made this discovery, thereby sharing with your listeners the excitement that is going to light up your guest's brain when they recount that story.

How Does This Actually Work in Podcasting?

Practically, how can you incorporate story structure into your podcast? Sometimes the story may play out in an obvious way, but other times, it may not seem like there's one at all. Here are some questions to help you find the story in your content:

- Why is this topic worth talking about? Why does it matter? Why will people care?
- Who are the main characters? Who are the people that listeners will care about or feel strongly about?
- What will listeners relate to in this story? How will listeners connect to what is being told?

Think of the best interviews you've seen or heard. They're not just a series of unconnected questions; in fact, they often follow this three-act structure. First, the interviewer may use questions to set the stage, establishing some important facts about the subject: "So, you've just had a baby, right?" or "You've just finished a new movie, haven't you?"

The interviewer will then introduce a conflict or dilemma, either serious or light-hearted: "But you didn't plan to become an actor, did you?" or "I hear this movie almost didn't get made?" or "A little bird tells me something crazy happened on set the first day of shooting." This sets the subject up to tell an interesting story or recount a challenge in their life. They may offer the resolution themselves or the interviewer might have to ask "How are you doing now?" or "Are the two of you still friends?"

If you are creating narrative radio, the story may be more obvious, like in my example of X the artist. But you can't assume the listener will find the story themselves. You have to use your editing skills to guide them on their listening journey.

For example, you may have an oral history recording of a coal worker talking about what it was like to work in the mines and how the industry changed. An anecdote about "how things were" is nice, but by selecting the right parts of this recording and filling in the gaps with narration and historical context, you can make him the main character in a story where the conflict is the change in the coal industry. How does he navigate this challenge? How have things resolved today? Did he get a new job? Did others? Are people still experiencing this same challenge?

The bottom line is that your podcast has to be entertaining. Each episode, whether it stands alone or is part of a series, *must* entertain your listeners and keep them coming back for more.

You cannot assume that someone will listen all the way to the end in order to hear the really interesting part or that they will listen to the first four episodes so that you can share the exciting turn of events in episode five. There's nothing stopping your listener from turning off the podcast and listening to the radio instead. They must be engaged and entertained.

The Introduction

A compelling podcast episode begins by grabbing the listener's attention in the first 90 seconds. Within that first minute and a half, podcasters need to convince their audience to keep listening. There are a few ways to do this.

Remember your elevator pitch from the first chapter? You can turn that into your opening lines for the podcast, using 20 seconds to let new listeners know what the show is about and why they should keep listening.

A popular way to make the first 90 seconds interesting is to include a "pull quote" from the main interview. This is a really great, concise clip from your tape that will get a reaction from the listener and make them want to find out more. Place it between the lines that open the show and the main episode content or at the very beginning of the episode.

If you have a particularly great story, you can jump in with a "cold open." You've probably seen this done in movies and television hundreds of times when the story begins immediately without any context or credits. Once this scene is established, you can "run your credits" or in this case, your intro music and opening lines.

I used this technique in my episode, "Memorial to an Eruption." The episode opens with the sound of gravel crunching and I tell the listeners that I am standing on a volcano. You can hear that I'm outdoors as I describe what I am seeing before telling you I'm going to head back down to the museum at the foot of the volcano "to learn about the eruption that devastated this tiny island." More gravel crunching transitions into the title sequence, where I play the main song for the episode along with my usual opening lines. Cold opens are used frequently by the stars of narrative radio to set the stage and make sure listeners need to know what happens next.

By the time you've finished an episode, it can be hard to evaluate it objectively and decide if the opening is going to hook new listeners. Try playing just the first 90 seconds for someone who hasn't heard the episode yet—or even better, someone who hasn't listened to the podcast at all. Ask them what they think about it? Would they keep listening? Why? If they weren't intrigued, why not? This is a good practice to help you develop opening segments that immediately grab your listener, making them excited to hear the rest of the episode.

Keeping the Audience Engaged

You've hooked your audience with your killer intro and first 90 seconds, but you still need to keep them focused and interested through the rest of the episode. There are a number of effective ways to do this, so let's focus on a few key techniques: editing, signposting, and creating a personal connection.

One of my favorite moments in the reality TV show *RuPaul's Drag Race* is in Season 5, Episode 1. While critiquing a drag queen who has included twice as many costume elements in her outfit as she needed, Ru says, "May I give you a word of advice? *Edit.*" I play that scene in my head every time I go to edit my interview tape.

Especially during my first few months of podcasting, I couldn't bear to cut anything out. Every part of the interview was interesting, and I didn't want my listeners to miss out on anything! What I didn't realize then was that I was actually achieving the opposite of my intended goal by publishing episodes that had too many topics, tangents, and lengthy scenes.

My episodes were, to put it bluntly, more boring than they needed to be. To avoid falling back into that bad habit of under-editing, I repeat my new mantra to myself every time I go to produce a new episode: "May I give you a word of advice? *Edit.*"

One of the hardest parts of being a director is knowing which scenes to cut. By keeping only the best and most relevant parts of your interviews, you ensure that the full impact of your episode doesn't get lost under too many unnecessary tassels and fringes—parts that are probably awesome, but just not for this episode.

A sure-fire path to boring your listeners is to let them get lost. Have you ever been listening to a radio program or podcast, zoned out for a minute, then realized you had no idea what was going on in the show? This is a big risk in podcasting since it's likely your audience is multitasking, doing chores or driving while listening.

To keep their minds from wandering off, you need to *signpost*.[5] If your interview subject mentions something obscure or jumps ahead chronologically, you can signpost for your listener by stopping your subject and asking them to explain or remind you who that person was. Otherwise, your listener may find themselves disengaging from the story to wonder "Am I supposed to know who that is?"

You can also create signposts in your script or narration by interrupting the interview tape to say something like, "Yes, that's right. They said zombies," or otherwise repeating and reinforcing what has just been said. This answers the question your listener may be asking ("Wait, did they just say zombies?") and ensures that they don't miss key facts or moments in the story, especially if those are necessary for understanding something that comes later in the episode.

Allie Ward, host of the podcast *Ologies*, is great at this. She interviews scientists and other highly educated specialists, and the jargon they use and the references they make are often too obscure for the average listener to pick up. So, Allie frequently stops the interview tape to give a little narration that fills you in on what has just been referenced or answers a question that was asked in passing (and might distract you if you don't get an answer).

Another way to draw your audience in and keep them listening is to make a personal connection. Historical interpreters do this all the time when they ask a personal question before a tour to engage the visitors and help them start making connections between their experience and the history being discussed.

---

[5] Although this was a technique I was already using, I didn't have a name for it until I read *Out On the Wire: The Storytelling Secrets of the New Masters of Radio* by Jessica Abel.

Used correctly, getting the audience to make a personal connection can really draw them into the story. The best example of this I've ever heard is from the podcast *Heaven's Gate*. The subject of the show is the strange cult of the same name that committed group-suicide in the 1990s in order to hitch a ride on a comet that they thought was a passing spaceship. That's not a very relatable group, and so most media stories about them engage audiences by furthering the sense of strangeness or un-relatability of the group members.

Instead, Glynn Washington, the host of *Heaven's Gate,* constantly finds ways to portray these cult members as individual humans. Having grown up in a cult himself, Washington leads this process of humanization by example, explaining to the audience that—even though it sounds crazy to kill yourself on the orders of your cult leader—he's only alive today because the leader of his doomsday cult didn't ask for that sacrifice. By this time, we the listeners have already connected with Washington, so this knowledge that our friend Glynn could have ended up like that is profound.

He takes the first step of empathy himself, and throughout the series, repeatedly invites the listener to consider what they have in common with the members of Heaven's Gate. Listening to this podcast, my personal life and beliefs became more and more connected to the story, and by the end, the podcast felt like a guided journey into exploring my own assumptions and unquestioned allegiances.

This is an extreme example of how to make these personal connections with your listener, but you can do it on a subtler level as well. By framing your story in a way that highlights universals (love, rejection, ambition, etc.) and using your narration or script to connect a distant topic to something closer to your listeners' lives, you can keep them engaged in the podcast on an emotional level.

Radio is a Visual Medium

"Radio is the most visual medium." This a line that gets used a lot among public radio producers, most notably by Ira Glass from *This American Life*. How can it be visual when it's literally only an auditory medium? Transom's Rob Rosenthal—paraphrasing Robert Krulwich—puts it this way:

> … when radio is produced well, the listener is a co-author. The idea being that when you read a book, an author provides clues as to what something looks like but the reader creates the images. In that way, the author and the reader work in tandem.[6]

In other words, you can provide a more vivid, immersive experience by using just the right amount of description that your listeners need in order to build their own mental pictures. Like in a great novel, too much description bogs down the story and the listener's imagination. You need to give them just the bare minimum they need to construct the rest of the image themselves.

In the episode of my podcast where I visit a famous writer's house (Season 1, Episode 3), it's important that the listener visualizes the environment around the home:

> The area around the Laxness House is still open and largely still undeveloped. Coming from Reykjavík, the bright white house and its cluster of trees is visible at the top of a long, sloping hill after you turn off of the main road…Signage for the museum stops at the parking area near the house, so as you walk up the driveway to the front door, there's nothing to suggest that this is anything other than a typical Icelandic family home.

I could have also told my listeners that the house was two stories with a mid-century design, that there was a small garage facing the driveway, that there

---

[6] Rosenthal, Rob. "Radio is a Visual Medium." *Transom*. December 12, 2017. https://transom.org/2017/radio-visual-medium/.

was a pool next to the house or any number of other details about the home and landscape. Instead, I wanted to give them just enough details to start building a picture themselves. It doesn't matter to the story whether they imagine a farmhouse or a modern structure. The important thing is that the house sits up on a hill, overlooking the area and that it's a landmark, visible from quite a way back.

When you are adding descriptions to your narration, think about what the audience needs to know and what they can imagine on their own.

Plan for the Ideal Story

If you want to tell a compelling story, it's easier to plan for that story than to try and tease it out of your tape after the interview. You can plan by researching your guests or subjects, brainstorming questions to ask, and drafting your ideal story. Do this *before* you gather your tape, and you'll be much better prepared to get the material you need.

What do I mean by ideal story? What would be the best outcome of an interview? Would it be perfect if they connected their work to a recent event that's in the news? Do you hope they will really unpack why they made a certain decision? Answering questions like these *before* you interview a guest helps you plan the ideal outcome. It may sound artificial to plan what you want your guest to say, but in fact, it's a skill that the world's best interviewers rely on to get those stories and insights that no one else can.

Before I visit a museum to record for *Museums in Strange Places*, I go through their entire website, noting down keywords and any interesting things I find. I usually also do a Google News search to find more information. However, since I'm often interviewing subjects at small museums that don't have a lot of information online, I do the bulk of my planning just before recording.

Before we begin the interview, I ask my host to give me a 15-minute tour of their museum. This accomplishes two things: it gives me the lay of the land, and it provides some time for me to develop a rapport with my subject. I use the information I get in those 15 minutes to make a quick mental map of the topics I want to cover and the order in which I want to address them. I'll also take note of any additional sounds or ambiance I want to capture while I am there.

If you are conducting interviews, this process can be as simple as chatting with your guest for ten minutes before you get started, asking a few prep-questions, and generally figuring out what they are most passionate about.

This strategy works for me almost every time. When a guest falls silent or gets nervous, I can use the information I already have to coax the story out of them. Since I know what tone I want to take and what note I want to end on, I can push them to articulate something that has only been alluded to. In this situation, I am the director—the expert—and I need to direct my interview subjects. I can't leave the quality of my show dependent on the variable of my guests' eloquence on any given day.

Often this is as simple as getting my subjects to restate something in a new way. They may have expressed a profound idea in a not-so-profound manner. If I ask the same question in a few different variations, I often get my key quote. Here are a few lines to try when your guest isn't quite getting to the core of what you want them to address:

- So, you are saying that…?
- In what way?
- Can you unpack that idea for me?
- How so?
- What's the big takeaway here?
- How would you explain that to someone who had never heard of x?
- I'm not sure I understand?

Wrapping Up

How do you end an episode in a memorable way? Again, there are so many creative ways to do this, but a great place to start is with a punchy end quote, a bit of reflection, or a big takeaway. This final moment is what will linger in your listener's mind and hopefully keep them thinking about the episode long after they finish listening. Just like you shouldn't wait until the end to reveal the interesting parts of the episode, you don't want to let the energy or focus peter out in the last few minutes.

Like a great piece of classical music leaves just the right final note lingering before the applause begins, look for the moment in your audio that has that sense of closure or finality. And if you don't have it in your tape, create it in your script.

Chapter 5
Launching Your Podcast

You've created an audio masterpiece! Now comes the fun part: sharing your podcast with the world. I want you to keep these principles in mind during each step of the launch process:

- Make it as easy as possible for people to find and listen to the podcast.
- Connect your institution's brand to the podcast brand whenever and wherever possible.
- Plan for success. Do not plan for failure.
- Share your excitement and passion for the project with everyone you can reach.
- Make sure that everyone—inside and outside your organization— knows that this podcast launch is a Big. Freaking. Deal.

Artwork and Description

Your podcast cover art and description are two of the most important factors potential listeners will use to determine whether or not they give your show a listen. Make sure they are great. Don't make them an afterthought!

Your artwork should be a 1400 x 1400 pixel square. That is the minimum size for Apple Podcasts and most other podcast platforms have the same requirements. The cover art should be readable and enticing in thumbnail size. That means if you shrink it down to 150 x 150 pixels, it should still look great. Most people will be seeing it at that size or smaller on their mobile devices, and that's where it will need to stand out.

I do not recommend using your logo as the cover art, although you should incorporate it into the cover art if possible to integrate the podcast brand and your institution's brand. If you have a graphic designer on staff, have them do the artwork, or hire a professional. This is not the place to save some money on a DIY design. For design inspiration, browse the top podcasts in your category on Apple Podcasts and save those cover images to create a "mood board" for your designer.

Spend some time on your description. This is your sales pitch to the world, your book jacket summary, your dating profile. It's your chance to make someone go, "Now that's something I have to hear." The first line of the description should be your hook. If you are feeling uninspired, go back to your elevator pitch from Chapter One and draw on that carefully crafted sales pitch to write your description. Let potential listeners know exactly what they will be getting if they subscribe to your show. (Same rules apply to the description of each individual episode).

Make sure your art and description reflect the podcast's creator: your institution. There's no point in creating a podcast for your organization if listeners aren't immediately able to make that connection.

Hosting & Distribution

You will need a podcast hosting service. Your media host is where your podcast files live; they literally "host" the mp3 for each episode. The hosting service will create an RSS feed that you can push out to Apple Podcasts, Google Podcasts, Stitcher, Overcast.fm, Spotify, and every other podcast listening platform in the world.

In case you were wondering, Apple Podcasts still counts for about 60% of all podcast listening in the world, so it should be your top priority when it comes to publishing.

It's critical that your podcast is on every listening platform possible. I have seen so many museums and cultural organizations go through all the work of creating a podcast, only to limit their sharing to Soundcloud, which makes up for a negligible percentage of podcast listens. Please don't do this.

Some of the top hosting services for podcasts are: Libsyn, Blubrry, Podbean, Spreaker, Audioboom, Buzzsprout, and Pippa. Soundcloud used to be a very popular hosting platform but has been largely replaced by services designed specifically for podcasting. You can compare prices and services on these platforms, and if you don't want that many choices to research, just choose between Libsyn and Blubrry.

Libsyn accounts for about 25% of the top 400 podcasts in the US, and it's the service I use to host *Museums in Strange Places*. They have a simple interface and a responsive support team. Hosting on Libsyn starts at about $7-$15 a month including statistics on downloads/listens, which you should make sure to get no matter which platform you use.

Libsyn (like most other hosting services) provides in-depth instructions on how to set up your podcast, so I'm not going to summarize those steps here. Before you get started, take an hour or two to familiarize yourself with your chosen hosting service by watching and reading any tutorials or FAQs they have.

Note that you will have to use Apple Podcasts Connect to get an iTunes destination link for your hosting service. Your host will have instructions on what they want and how to get it. Make sure to review the instructions on pushing your RSS feed out to other podcast listening platforms. There will be a few listed (on Libsyn, they are under "Destinations"), but many platforms, including Google Podcasts, will pick up your RSS feed automatically.

PodLink (https://pod.link/) is a cool new website that will show direct links to all the top listening platforms your podcast is on. Test it out by searching for "*Museums in Strange Places,*" and you'll get a set of links to my podcast's homepage on the top podcast apps and websites.

You can set up your hosting account at any point, but your podcast won't be visible on Apple Podcasts and other listening platforms until you have published your first episode. We'll get into the question of when to publish Episode 1 as we discuss the launch.

Website & Show Notes

Your podcast needs a good online home. It doesn't have to be fancy, just one easy-to-find place where listeners can find out more about the show, see which podcast listening platforms it's on, and so on.

Keeping in mind that your podcast branding should be deeply connected to that of your institution, this online home should be part of your existing website. If you cannot include it on your existing website, create a simple Wordpress or Squarespace site, make it look as similar to your existing site as possible, and make sure it drives listeners to your home page (and vice versa).

The podcast homepage should be easily locatable from your main home page. Don't hide your podcast! Remember, as far as the podcast team is concerned, this is the most important thing happening in the museum, so try and give it the placement and attention it deserves.

Most podcasts release "show notes" for each episode. These are entries or posts on the podcast's website or homepage that usually includes these elements:

- The episode description
- At least one or two images
- Links to any music or other elements that need credit
- Links to things discussed or mentioned in the episode that listeners may want to know more about

- Links to podcast listening platforms
- Anything else you want!

Your show notes are a great place to lead curious listeners to relevant items in your collections or upcoming programs, turning their love of your podcast into direct engagement with your institution. A great set of show notes is a useful tool for sharing new episodes. Make sure there's a great cover image that will grab the attention of potential listeners on social media.

Accessibility & Transcription

Your show notes are also the place you should include a transcript of each episode if you plan to include one. Transcripts are essentially scripts of your show that:

- Make your podcast accessible to those who are deaf and hard-of-hearing.
- Allow researchers to refer back to episodes more easily (if applicable to your show).
- Aid non-native speakers of your language in following the audio and practicing their language acquisition.

While the second two benefits are "nice things to have," making podcasts accessible to the deaf and hard-of-hearing community is a much more important matter of accessibility. If you can provide transcripts, I highly recommend doing so. State clearly on podcast materials that transcripts are available, because many deaf and hard-of-hearing podcast fans may want to check them out and won't know to look for the transcripts unless you advertise their existence.

You can create transcripts manually or use a service to have them done automatically. Doing them manually can be time-consuming if you have an unscripted show, but if you are already scripting the majority of your episodes, turning those scripts into transcriptions won't require too much extra effort. Some podcasters use Wreally's transcription tool to make the work go faster (https://transcribe.wreally.com/).

Some of the more popular services for podcast transcription are Rev (https://www.rev.com/, $1 per minute). Another service used in the field is Temi (https://www.temi.com/, 10 cents per minute), but it requires a lot more manual correction. I've also heard good things about Trint (https://trint.com/, $15 per hour). There is no perfect solution currently out there but experiment with these and other available services to find a solution that works for your podcast.

Generating Launch Buzz

It may be tempting to focus all your energy on simply making the podcast, but as I like to say, "'If you build, they will come'—is not a marketing strategy."

Neglecting to start strong with a big marketing push (and continuing to market your podcast after that) does a huge disservice to the incredible show you have created. With over 555,000 active podcasts out there, you'll have to put in a little work to let your ideal listeners know you exist. The good news is that you don't have to spend a lot of money to do that! There are plenty of inexpensive marketing tactics you can use for the launch to make sure your podcast hits the ground running.

First, create a trailer. As I mentioned before, your podcast will not be live on podcast platforms until you publish your first episode. It can take up to a few days for your very first episode to be approved on Apple Podcasts (after that, they should show up almost immediately after you hit publish). A trailer lets you work through that initial publishing process and set a firm release date for episode one.

Your trailer doesn't have to be fancy! It's actually really easy to produce a great trailer for audio. Just pick some of the best short clips from your first few episodes and put them over some good ambient music. Include a short bit of narration: "Coming soon from the Local Museum, a podcast about the fascinating stories hidden in our community." At the end of the trailer, you can put a call to action: "Subscribe on Apple Podcasts, Google Podcasts, or wherever you get your podcast fix. Episode one drops on August 10." The whole trailer should be under two minutes. For a great example of how to do this, look at the trailers the SF MoMA has released for each season of their podcast *Raw Material.*

Use your trailer to generate buzz before the podcast even launches. Building a podcast audience can take time, but if you plan ahead, you'll be off to a strong start. Think of your podcast launch like a movie premiere. You want to attract potential listeners before the first episode is released so that they will excitedly download it on day one. To do this, you should assemble a launch team.

I learned the launch team tactic from the book *Published.*, by Chandler Bolt. Bolt is teaching his readers how to launch their self-published book, but the lessons can easily be applied to a podcast launch. In fact, podcasts are basically self-published radio. Here's how he describes a great launch team:

> In a nutshell, your launch team is a group of people, hand picked by you, who are eager to help market and make your book launch a triumph. Because they believe in you and your book, this team is going to give their time, ideas, skills, and networks to ensure that your book launch is a success.

Just substitute "podcast" for "book," and you have your launch team. The great news for museums, history organizations, and cultural nonprofits is that you likely already have staff, volunteers, and regular visitors who love what you do and want to support you.

Invite people to apply for the launch team using a Google form. Send the ask out to your current volunteers, followers on social media, your general email lists, and staff members who aren't already involved in the podcast. 150 to 250 launch team members is a good number to shoot for, but don't worry if you have less.

Organize your launch team through a dedicated email list and a private Facebook group. Aim to have the launch team built about two weeks before the trailer drops. You'll release the first episode two to three weeks after that. Give your launch team regular tasks to keep them engaged and excited (but not overwhelmed or overworked), using the Facebook group and/or email list to reward them with behind the scenes photos and other goodies.

Ask your launch team to help you with these types of things:

- Downloading the trailer and sharing it and other pre-launch news on their own social media pages
- Reaching out to any contacts they may have at local radio stations, newspapers, blogs, etc. to get press coverage of the trailer and first episode
- Contacting people at other organizations who would be interested in the podcast and in promoting it through their own channels
- Leaving reviews on iTunes/Apple Podcasts when the trailer and episode one are released
- Downloading the first episode on the day it comes out and sharing it with everyone they know

You don't have to limit the excitement to online platforms. Why not have a launch party where your fans and all the hard-working members of your launch team can listen to the first episode together? Release episode one in the morning, and have the launch party in the afternoon or evening, for example. Make sure there are lots of things to keep people from getting bored while you "screen" the episode; have relevant coloring pages, adult crafts, party food (chips and dips, etc.), and comfortable chairs. Have a Q&A afterward with the show's creators. Invite local journalists, bloggers, and other influencers to the launch party to make sure word gets out about the new podcast.

Ongoing Marketing

After you hit the ground running with a powerful launch, you'll need to keep marketing! Schedule marketing time into your schedule for every episode. If you don't like marketing, just schedule time to share what you've made with people who will love it. Here are some ways you can grow your podcast audience:

Use your email lists. Send out an email whenever a new episode drops. Include some extra information on the subject or other things that will make that a fun email to open.

Keep sharing on social media. Share each episode on your institution's social media accounts. Don't create separate accounts or profiles for the podcast. Use your existing reach and authority to get the podcast out there. If you can, set aside $20 for each episode to run Facebook ads and get it to new listeners.

Write to local news media and bloggers who might be interested in the subject of each episode. I personally had great success growing my audience during Season 1 of *Museums in Strange Places* by writing online articles about each episode for an English-language culture magazine in Iceland. I gave them free online content; they shared my podcast with their 70,000 followers.

Are you a member of any associations? They will be thrilled to hear that one of their members has created a podcast. They probably also need content for their email newsletters and social media. Send them your podcast! Many associations also have magazines that feature and review member projects.

Apply for awards. I guarantee there are plenty of awards in your field. The American Alliance of Museums has a special "Podcast" category for their MUSE Media & Technology Awards (*Museums in Strange Places* won an award in that category in 2018). The American Association for State and Local History has an annual awards program that has included podcasts in the past. The National Council on Public History also has an awards program. Penguin Random House has a Library Award for Innovation. The American Library Association has an awards program. You can also look for city or state-based awards. Apply for any award you can find! Having an award-winning podcast makes it easier to secure guests, get funding, and open more doors for promoting your show.

If you have guests on your show, ask them to promote their episode with their own networks (and remind them if they forget to do it). Make sure they have links and images and an episode description on hand.

Let's Talk about Money

This book is all about creating a killer podcast on a budget, but I understand that even a few hundred dollars for equipment and the cost dedicated staff time might be a stretch for many of you. I've included multiple tiers of cost in most chapters, but I want to talk explicitly here about funding and saving money.

First, let's talk about "the ask." You'll need to ask your superiors, board, or stakeholders for the green light to make a podcast. Prepare for this ask by perfecting your elevator pitch, anticipating questions about production (using what you have learned in this book), and having statistics about podcast listener engagement on-hand. I recommend using my *Podcast Pitch Template* from the *Worksheet and Template Bundle* to create a printed report (no more than a few pages long). Pitch the podcast then give any decision-makers a copy of the report to read after your initial conversation.

In your pitch, you will need to include a budget. You can find a customizable *Podcast Budget Template* in the *Worksheet and Template Bundle*. Use it to create a budget that reflects the true costs to your organization.

If the money just can't be found in your institution's budget, there are a few other avenues to explore. If you already have a donor-base, consider making the podcast pitch directly to a long-term donor. Depending on their interests, they may enjoy getting a producer credit or being involved in the podcast in some way.

Alternatively, you can aim for more donors giving small amounts by crowd-funding the project. A third option is to create a podcast that a large donor or a large group of small donors want to hear. This means handing over some of the creative control in developing the concept.

Once you have built your podcast audience, you can also ask podcast listeners to donate a small monthly amount to keep the podcast going. This is a method used by many podcasters; it usually requires a large number of small donations, so I wouldn't recommend relying on this method as a primary funding source until you have a larger audience.

Networks and other big podcasting players like Spotify and Google are increasingly offering resources, training, and platforms for people of color and other less-represented groups interested in making podcasts. If the individuals making the podcast for your institution qualify for these types of programs, you may be able to get some world-class training for free to take back to your institution.

Sponsorship is one of the most common ways many podcasters fund their show. If you have a compelling pitch and plan to grow your audience, you can get sponsors before you launch. Getting sponsors is like making sales calls. You'll need to call or email businesses that want to reach your audience, pitch your amazing show, and tell them how much it will cost to sponsor each episode or a whole season. Use my *Sponsor Pitch Slides Sample* to create a slide deck and the *Sponsor Pitch Cover Letter Sample* to craft an accompanying email.

To make sure your sponsors get a return on their investment, you should mention their sponsorship at the beginning and end of the episode and create a 20-second ad at the beginning or first third of your podcast. The 20-second spot should thank them for their generous support of this podcast, tell audience members what they do and how to find them, and offer a call-to-action for listeners who want to use their products or services. Also, include a link to your sponsor's website in the episode description and on your show notes page.

A lot of podcasters try to support their show by selling merchandise (t-shirts, buttons, etc.). This is a great way to create a more dedicated fan-base, but it's not a good way to support the podcast (at least on its own). You'll earn very little on merchandise relative to the work that will go into it.

Last, but not least, let's talk about saving money by tapping into your community. Are there experts in your institution's network who would donate their skills and time to the project? Are there favors you can call in? Can you share recording equipment with another institution who wants to podcast? Better yet, are there free or low-cost recording studios in your city that you can use? (You'd be surprised how many of these are out there). Get creative!

What Does Success Look Like?

So you've launched your podcast. Now how do you measure its success? What does success even look like?

The easiest place to look for validation is your download numbers. Of course, it's exciting to see how many times the show has been downloaded, but I would encourage you to find other ways to measure the success of the show besides reaching a certain number.

Unfortunately, there isn't a standard way to measure and report on downloads across podcast-listening platforms. Some include automatic downloads, some don't; some only count downloads on certain devices; some count plays rather than downloads; and some cache your podcast, making it hard for a stats aggregator like Libsyn to see how many downloads they are actually providing. Your download numbers should be considered a rough estimate. So, that said, how many downloads can you expect?

The best standard for measuring relative downloads are the monthly numbers released by Libsyn via their podcast, *The Feed*. They fluctuate every month, but not so much that you can't use one month's stats to generalize a longer period of time. Here are the July 2018 numbers from Libsyn-hosted podcasts (compiled by the invaluable *podnews* newsletter, which you can subscribe to at https://podnews.net/):

> If you have over 142 downloads of an episode in 30 days you're doing better than 50% of all podcasts on Libsyn. If you have 1,200 downloads, you're doing better than 80%; 3,300 90%; 8,100 95%; 19,000 98%; 32,000 99%.

142 may sound like a really small number compared to more familiar stats like views on Facebook or Youtube videos, but podcasting is a "slower" medium than online video. While the 3,000 views on your Facebook video include every user who slows down to watch a few seconds before moving on, Edison Research's *2018 Infinite Dial Study* revealed that 80% of podcast listeners hear all or most of each episode they consume.

Compare your download numbers to live events rather than other online stats. If you had 150 engaged attendees at a program, would you consider it a success?

The most important thing you can learn from your podcasts stats is whether your audience is growing. The measurement you want to identify is the number of downloads each episode gets in the first 30 days after it is published. If that number is growing each episode, it's safe to say your audience is growing.

By the way, you'll be able to pick up new audience members faster by publishing every week or every other week. I know it's not always possible to meet that kind of schedule, but just know that if you are releasing once a month, it's going to take a lot longer to see that growth. Consider releasing episodes every other week during your season, and then having a longer break between seasons rather than releasing monthly if you are concerned with slow growth.

What other ways can you measure the success of your podcast? Well first and foremost, remember those goals you set at the beginning of this book? Are those goals being met? If the podcast has thousands of downloads for every episode, but those goals aren't being met, maybe it's time to rethink how you are using the podcast to reach those goals.

Are people leaving reviews and getting in touch to share how much they like the podcast? Save every one of those notes. They are worth far more than downloads in evaluating the podcast's impact. Listener feedback measures one of the most important goals of podcasting: putting on a show that people enjoy.

How to Actually Do This

There's a lot of information in this book. (In fact, I could have written another five chapters on the ins and outs of podcasting.) But don't feel overwhelmed! Almost everyone who podcasts today started out having no idea what they were doing. It's a field filled with amateurs and experimenters. Use the rules in this book or ditch my rules and make your own if you find a better way to do things. If your podcast is great and people are listening, *that's all that matters.*

I guarantee that along the way, you will feel moments of intense doubt and succumb to bouts of imposter syndrome. You'll think, "I can't do this, why did I think I could do this?"

I'm giving you permission to lie on the floor and mope for 10 minutes. Then pick yourself back up and just keep working. There's this horrible stage in creating an episode where all the elements are there, but it's still a mess. It's so intimidating and sometimes it seems impossible that this mess could be turned into a great episode. These are the moments where I face crushing doubt and want to give up. Then I get back to work, and—within a few hours—a great podcast episode emerges from the jumble of audio.

I attended the Podcast Movement conference in 2018. The sessions were great and I learned a lot. But the most valuable thing I got from the whole week was being around other active podcasters. To be a podcaster, you have to face down the roadblocks of self-doubt and perfection every week. Many podcasters are creating their shows from home, working alone.

What separates those who want to podcast from these folks—who are actually podcasting—is the ability to work with a deadline and publish episodes that aren't perfect. Your episodes will never be perfect. You might be tempted to compare yourself to *This American Life* or *Radiolab*; did you know these podcasts are made by *teams* who spend an insane amount of time producing the smallest story?

You don't have a whole day to dedicate to fine-tuning the script for a five-minute piece, so you're probably not going to be the next *This American Life*. That doesn't mean you can't make something great. Just keep podcasting, and you *will* get better. Use every episode to improve *one* aspect of the show (scripting, interviews, scoring, etc.).

Don't do it alone! Even if you are the only person working on this project, ask colleagues, friends, or family to listen to episodes before they go out if you are nervous. I still ask my husband to listen to almost every episode before I hit publish. Hearing feedback from a supportive person you trust is the best cure for self-doubt and imposter syndrome.

You can also find support online. There are lots of podcasts dedicated to podcasting (*HowSound* is my favorite) and Facebook groups full of podcasters at every level. Podcast Movement has a great Facebook group and if you are a woman, woman-identifying, or non-binary, stop what you are doing right now and join the She Podcasts Facebook group. I also recommend signing up for the *podnews* email newsletter (https://podnews.net/), a daily email that will keep you updated on the podcasting world and the many resources available.

And don't forget to download all the free worksheets and templates I've created to go with this book at http://hhethmon.com/BookBonus

Need More Help?

And hey, I'm here if you need more help! I offer guidance and instruction at every level, from hourly coaching calls to three-day intensive workshops. Visit hhethmon.com/services to learn more and book a free 15-minute consultation to discuss your podcast idea.

Together we can adapt the information from this book (and more) to your institution's unique needs and ensure that your podcast project is a success.

If you want more intensive instruction, why not host a Podcast Masterclass Workshop? I will travel to your institution and put on a three-day intensive workshop for your podcast team. If you are serious about launching a successful podcast or revamping your existing show, this workshop is a must. Visit http://hhethmon.com/services/workshop to learn more and book your workshop.

Please let me know about your podcast once it is launched. I want to promote the heck out of it to all my followers and add it to the directory of podcasts by museums, history organizations, and cultural nonprofits on my website at hhethmon.com/podcastdirectory.

Appendix
Alternatives to Producing In-House

Creating a podcast entirely in-house is a big undertaking. I think many museum professionals can rise to the challenge, but I realize that not everyone has the time. Here are a few alternatives to doing it all yourself.

Hiring an Editor

A podcast editor takes your raw material (interview audio, script, music), and puts it all together. Since editing is a big time-drain for beginners, hiring an editor can save you a lot of time. Hiring an editor will start at $50-100 for a 30-minute episode and can get up to a few thousand per episode.

The price will depend on how much work the editor needs to do. Is this just an interview show that needs an intro and some clean-up throughout, or is this a more complicated narrative that requires multiple pieces being assembled in a specific order? The more you expect the editor to do for you (and the better their ear), the more they will cost.

To find an editor, I recommend asking for referrals in podcasting groups online or from other podcasters. Googling will get you a lot of online services that offer to do everything for a monthly fee. While these may be worth trying, you'll get a more customized service from an independent editor. To determine whether they are a good fit for your show, listen to other shows they've edited and see if you like their work.

Hiring a Production Company

A production company can come in and lead the podcast process from concept to publication. Working with a production company means trading money for expertise and time.

While researching this section, I spoke with the founders of Chalk & Blade, a UK-based group with experience producing podcasts for museums. If you have a high-profile institution, hiring a production company can ensure that your podcast has a slick professional sound to match your existing brand. Or maybe you have a great idea, but don't want the burden of turning the idea into reality to fall on staff members.

Companies like Chalk & Blade will customize their services to fit the needs and abilities of the client institution. What are you willing to do yourself in order to reduce the budget and what requires an outside expert? Do you want to do the interviews and narration yourself, or will you be hiring a host to represent your museum?

If you want to explore this option, see who has produced the podcasts at the big institutions in your field. Once you have identified a few production companies that are doing the kind of work you are interested in, listen to the shows they have produced. No matter how well a company pitches their services, it's the quality of their previous work that will let you know whether they are worth hiring.

Partnering with Public Radio

Partnering with your local public radio station can be a great way to create a podcast (and get lots of exposure) without having to produce the episode in-house. The Philbrook Museum of Art in Oklahoma partnered with Public Radio Tulsa to create *Museum Confidential*, a behind-the-scenes look at museums hosted by the Philbrook's Jeff Martin. The MoMA collaborated

YOUR MUSEUM NEEDS A PODCAST

with New York Public Radio's WNYC Studios on a ten-episode podcast on art with celebrity host Abbi Jacobson and celebrity guests like Questlove and RuPaul.

Working with a Third Party in the Community

Though it requires a bit more pre-planning, you can also invite a third-party from your community to create a podcast about your museum or using your museum. Maybe an artist is interested in creating a podcast about the strange objects in your collection. Perhaps an activist group wants to talk about decolonizing your museum. Could you invite a theater group to create an audio-drama about your institution or its collections?

You can offer these third parties access to your collections, staff, and other behind-the-scenes spaces and information. You can also offer them a wider audience and the credibility of an institutional brand. The level of creative control you have over these collaborations will depend on what arrangement you come to. Make sure to really think through this type of collaboration before going ahead with one. Who will be liable? Who will control the publishing of the episodes? Who will own the rights to the final products?

Get Coaching for In-House Production and Hiring Third Parties

If you want someone to guide you through the process of doing it yourself or hiring specialists, I offer flexible consulting packages. You can get scheduled calls whenever you need them to go over questions, make sure you are on the right track, and get help choosing an editor or producer for your project. Visit http://hhethmon.com/services to learn more and book a free 15-minute consultation to discuss your podcasting needs.

Looking for More Advanced Podcast Training? Book a Podcast Masterclass Workshop at Your Institution

I will travel to you, anywhere in the world, and hold an intensive three-day workshop for your staff members or dedicated volunteers.

Through this intimate learning experience, you will:

- Refine your podcast concept and align it with your institutional goals.
- Plan out your first six episodes.
- Learn how to use podcasting equipment specifically chosen for your needs (and budget).
- Get hands-on training in editing and production.
- Expert guidance on hiring editors, producers, or other third-party experts (if needed).
- Develop a launch plan and a long-term marketing plan to ensure your podcast is a success.

What are you waiting for?

Make sure your institution isn't missing out on the power of podcasting. Visit **http://hhethmon.com/services** to schedule a free 15-minute consultation with me to discuss booking this workshop at your institution. Just include "I am interested in booking a workshop," in the form when scheduling your call.

ABOUT THE AUTHOR

Hannah Hethmon is a museum communications consultant and the producer of *Museums in Strange Places*, an award-winning podcast that explores the world through its museums. She is a native of the greater Washington, D.C. area and holds an M.A. in Medieval Norse Studies from the University of Iceland. Hannah grew up traveling the world with her family, living in Saudi Arabia, Egypt, and Canada. She still has that drive to explore the world and has recently lived in Iceland, Denmark, and Poland. She currently lives in Europe with her husband. Hannah is passionate about helping museums communicate effectively and meaningfully with their audiences. Find her on Twitter and Instagram @hannah_rfh or on her website: http://hhethmon.com.

36448371R00063

Printed in Poland
by Amazon Fulfillment
Poland Sp. z o.o., Wrocław